Backyard Adventure

Backyard Adventure

How to Create Outdoor Play Spaces for Kids

by

Paula Brook

The Globe Pequot Press

Chester, Connecticut

To Shaw, Abby & Shira

Updated in Fall 1990

Copyright © 1988 by Paula Brook

Photographs on pages 104, 134, 138, 148, 150, 159, and 169 by Krisitn Mullally; remaining photographs provided by the author. Illustrations by Liz Mowrey.

Library of Congress Cataloging-in-Publication Data

Brook, Paula.
    Backyard adventure: how to create outdoor play spaces for kids / by Paula Brook.—1st ed.
      p. cm.
    Reprint. Originally published: Moscow, Idaho : Solstice Press, 1988.
      Includes bibliographical references and index.
    ISBN 0-87106-359-X
    1. Play—United States. 2. Creative activities and seat work.
3. Games. I. Title.
[HQ782.B76 1990]   90-39436
649'.5—dc20   CIP

Manufactured in the United States of America
First Edition/Second Printing

Contents

Introduction   ix

1. Children Need To Play   1
What the experts say about children at play: Why children need to play; How children need to play; What parents need to do to let children play; Planning to avoid conflict

2. The Ground Rules   15
Design and safety considerations for backyard play: Suitable impact surfaces, retaining structures, storage, and rules that kids can live with

3. Making The Most of It   27
Ideas for small play spaces; Solutions for groundcover and contour problems, and some points on plants

4. Finding Loose Parts   39
How to survey the shops, tap community resources, browse the lumberyards and beat the bushes to build up a collection of "constructive playthings"

5. Building the Basics   53
Tools and tips for big and little hands: Detailed instructions on making versatile loose parts out of wood, rope, tires and found treasures

6. King of the Castle   75
Climbers, playhouses and tree forts: How to shop for backyard mega-toys; Plans for building the best and safest homemade alternatives; Deciding on swings, slides, ladders, ropes and pulleys

7. **World's Best Tomato**   105

Garden projects for growing kids: Preparing and plotting a garden a child can tend; Tools and rules; Windowsill, big pot and small plot projects

8. **Sandicrafts**   121

How to promote creative sand play in large and small spaces; Keeping it clean; Best boxes and alternatives; Water tables, pumps, pipes and streams

9. **The Backyard Scientist**   135

Intimate observations of ordinary things: Equipping the lab; Ideas for collecting and preserving; Learning about time, clouds, birds, worms, insects and snails

10. **Artsplay**   151

Backyard adventures in the arts: Equipping an outdoor studio; Plans for an easel; Recipes for modelling, sculpting and painting materials; Big and little ideas for outdoor painting, printing, puppets and dolls; Outdoor drama, music and noise

Appendices   171

Bibliography   178

Acknowledgments

W hen I started researching this book I had no idea how many truly inspired people have devoted their lives to the field of children's play. When I first stumbled across the term "play professional," I conjured up the image of some Disney-like caricature who spends his days tinkering with windup toys.

Then I met the real people—those who rally communities around the reconstruction of a derelict playground, who spend their days leading inner-city play groups and their evenings training new leaders to carry on the work, who build beautiful play equipment in tiny basement workshops, who quietly work for organizations like The International Association for the Child's Right to Play—most of whom get paid little or nothing for what they do. They simply do it because they care a great deal about children.

I am indebted to the following for providing both material and emotional inspiration: Valerie Fronczek of the Children's Play Resources Center in Vancouver, Gary Pennington of the Lord Roberts playground redevelopment committee, Louise Dean and Craig Campbell of Vancouver Community Workshop, landscape architect and playground designer Cornelia Hahn Oberlander, Wanda Justice of the Berwick Center Preschool, Peter Ashmore of Information Daycare Services and Barbara Hendricks of The Playground Network.

Thanks also to the many families who welcomed me into their backyards to observe, take pictures and sip lemonade.

Introduction

"There was a child went forth every day,
And the first object he looked upon, that object he became,
And that object became part of him for the day or a certain part of the day,
Or for many years or stretching cycles of years...."

Walt Whitman

W alt Whitman's lines have taken on intense new meaning for me since beginning work on this book. I was hardly a stranger to children in the first place, with two youngsters of my own and a library stuffed with reference aids from Adler to Spock. But it wasn't until I started researching my subject in earnest that I began to appreciate the full meaning of play.

I know what you're thinking. Play is simply play. Kids do it. Adults don't need to analyze it. Right?

You may be thinking the same way about your backyard. The kids are going to play there (no doubt quite contentedly) whether it looks like a miniaturized amusement park or the town dump. So why all the fuss?

Because there is serious reason to be concerned about the quality of children's play these days, which is really about the quality of their lives — after all, that's what kids do most of the time. At least, *play* is what a child is cut out to do. He is supposed to go out every day to "look upon" new things, to manipulate and change them and in turn be changed by them, thereby making the world part of himself and himself part of the world.

The most important thing a child will do his entire life is play. It is his very first lesson in the pursuit of self-knowledge, and the only way he can carry it out is on his own time and in his own fashion. Play ends when he begins pursuing someone else's goals by living up to parents' or teachers' expectations. Naturally, the time will come when he will have to face such responsibilities, but if he has had plenty of time to develop a positive view of himself and the world, he will be equipped to face them in an equally positive manner.

"To develop they must play," writes Polly Hill, a leading advocate in an international movement dedicated to the child's right to play. "Today children live in an urban environment that doesn't encourage play and is almost hostile to their development. It must be altered and controlled to meet their needs, and adults are the only ones who can do it."

I grew up in a charmed world—or so it seems when I look back at the small prairie city where neighborhoods (at least the ones I knew) were safe to play in, where best friends walked hand-in-hand to elementary school with their little brothers and sisters in tow, where my backyard was your backyard and moms in jam-stained aprons occasionally looked out kitchen windows to do a head count.

My kids are growing up in a different world. Car pools, carefully scheduled trips to the playground, and "street-proofing" have replaced a good deal of the spontaneous adventure that is supposed to be at the core of childhood. I can't in good conscience open my back door and tell my kids to "go out and play" the way my mom used to. At least not without making sure the gates are latched and the kids swear a solemn oath not to open them.

But there is an alternative—backyard adventure. Your backyard can easily combine most, if not all, of the essential ingredients of active, spontaneous, creative play. It can solve the chief dilemma of family life in the fast lane—the conflict between the pressing need for control and for mutual independence. (We owe it not only to our children, but to ourselves, as a reward for the many hours we spend meeting their physical and emotional needs.) By creating a safe, yet challenging, play area in your own backyard, you can have it both ways.

It is difficult to address the needs of children of all ages when discussing play. Obviously children's needs and interests change radically from the toddler stage to the preteen years. Your yard should be able to meet those changing demands.

It is my goal to help you through the transitions. To do so I offer design strategies, equipment options and activities for children aged two to twelve, though there is no question that tiny infants and worldly teenagers can also benefit from any backyard improvements that may be kindled by this book.

No one knows your children better than you. Please adapt my ideas to their special interests and abilities. At times I may err on the side of caution with recommended age limits for certain activities, such as junior carpentry, and types of equipment, such as climbing structures. If you have faith in your four-year-old's hammering skills, or her Tarzan-like-climbing abilities, you are probably safe bending the rules. The opposite is also true: If your child is uncomfortable with physical challenges—don't push him.

Strict adherence to the rules for safe play and for safe equipment construction are most crucial for parents or other care givers responsible for groups of children. To date, in North America, there is little uniformity in play space requirements for day-care centers or public play areas. In many communities, virtually anyone can operate an unlicensed, unsupervised care facility with no adherence to safety code, and which promotes no particular play philosophy.

I hope this book adds to the small but growing movement to remedy this social malady. Even more important, whether you use it as a guide to redesigning your whole yard or as a source for occasional games and activities, I hope *Backyard Adventure* provides at least a little challenge and a whole lot of fun.

Children Need To Play

I f you are looking at a big, empty backyard or a small, barren patio, consider yourself lucky. That yawning space is just waiting to be transformed into a garden of earthly (and imaginary) delights.

Shut your eyes and picture the scene on an idyllic summer afternoon: a couple of kids rapt in concentrated pail-and-shovel work in the sandbox; another singing loudly while she swings; a teenager or two sprawling in the hammock with sci-fi novels and raspberry soda; and the twins from next door busily stringing up a pulley system joining their treehouse with yours.

I know what you're thinking. A simple phone call to the local department store will transform that open space into a play haven equipped with a swing set, maybe some monkey bars, a sandbox and a paddling pool for good measure. Then the backyard will be *complete*. No more fuss.

But don't do it. At least not yet. Sit down, the whole lot of you, and think about your potential play area—not as a problem, but rather as an untapped resource. If you find yourself overwhelmed by the possibilities, make an active decision to do absolutely nothing with the space for now. Take a whole summer—a year, if you want—to consider your priorities and resources.

First, take stock of the toys and equipment you already have. Then look around the neighborhood. If the kids across the lane have an all-in-one climber replete with swings, slides, bells, whistles and crow's nest lookout, you needn't install the same monster in your yard. If there is a park with a playing field nearby, you certainly won't need a soccer field of your own.

Now think about your family. Consider the ages of your children, the frequency and age-range of visitors to the yard, and the manner in which your kids play. Do they generally cooperate, or do they manage better given separate spaces and pastimes? Do they enjoy busy work at the activity table, playing shipwrecked pirates, or chasing the dog around and around the tree?

And don't forget yourself. How much of your neatly manicured lawn are you willing to cover with pea gravel or devote to an adventure scrap heap? If all you have is a terrace or patio, are you willing to crowd your barbecue equipment and lawn chairs to make room for a bulky sandbox?

Then examine your nerves. How high can your children climb before you find yourself hyperventilating beside the phone, fingers twitching over the 911 keys? Have you updated your householders' liability insurance? How much is all of this going to cost?

Why Children Need to Play

"If you really want to see what kids like to do best, bring them down to my place and let them loose in the bush," is the advice I got from a top-ranking urban playground designer. Employed by the city, he commutes to work, leaving his wife and children to enjoy rural life on a gulf island off the British Columbia coast. His backyard is literally bush. There his children build their own forts out of scrap lumber, fish in a nearby stream, safely operate their own BB-gun range and occasionally surface for meals.

Too often, especially in our cities, parents replace opportunities for active play with frenetic schedules of "educational" activities—gym, piano, ballet, swimming, art—all of which result in such a tremendous drain on the pocketbook and the gas tank. After heroic expenditures of money and time, many of us conclude we've put out as much as can be expected in the interest of our children's welfare.

The sad irony is that much greater satisfaction can be had all around for much less bother and expense. By keeping our children busy with such activities, we are in effect keeping them entertained. The minute they get bored, we find new forms of entertainment for them. With all the best intentions, we are failing miserably to provide them with the means of entertaining themselves, of developing their own resources and gaining self-esteem. The main thing they need is complete time off from our own busy schedules and high expectations—time off for play.

"What is absolutely clear is that we must give back to children what we have taken away from them, things which with a little imagination they can make something out of," says Swedish children's advocate Eva Noren-Bjorn. "If we do not do this, we will bring up children who already when young are passive consumers demanding entertainment rather than active individuals with a creative relationship to the world around them."

Given free time, space to move, and a variety of simple toys and things they can manipulate, explore and change to suit their momentary whims, children will play. It's in their nature. Unfortunately, they must rely on adults to provide these play opportunities. When we fail to do so, we not only rob them of fun, but we may be keeping them from growing into fully competent people, because play fosters learning and the development of skills needed for adult life.

To guide our children toward productive, satisfying lives as adults, we must first help them learn to express themselves, to respect their own and their playmates' achievements, to set their own limits and then reach beyond them to ever greater challenges.

How Children Need To Play

When experts talk about the developmental value of play, certain key words keep coming up—foremost is *adventure*.

The theory of "adventure play" originated in Europe and England after World War II, when urban planners and educators were faced with the challenge of creating play opportunities for inner-city children amid the postwar disorder and rubble. Derelict lots and barren alleys were their only resources. So adults claimed them, filled them with "beautiful junk," such as wood scraps, tires and piles of dirt, then let the children loose (under the supervision of "play leaders") to create their own playgrounds.

Observers soon realized that a liability had been turned to definite advantage in these shabby-looking adventure playgrounds. The children were thriving. Parents

3

were pleased. Community leaders were amazed at the hefty returns on such a modest investment.

"Most young people, at one time or another, have a deep urge to experiment with earth, fire, water and timber, to work with real tools without fear of undue criticism or censure," commented Lady Allen of Hurtwood, grandam of British playground designers. Give them the raw materials and let them create their own play, she maintained. Let them roast their own hot dogs over open fires, using sticks they've whittled with honest-to-goodness pocket knives. Resist the urge to structure their experiences. Supervise them, but from a distance.

Throughout the following decades Lady Allen, along with a small but dedicated group of children's advocates, pushed for a continuation of this ideal despite changing economics and urban aesthetics. To their credit, the tradition has survived in England, where close to ninety-five percent of public recreation budgets are spent on people—among them, a well-trained army of adventure playground supervisors.

The idea never got a toehold in North America, despite the best efforts of people like Cornelia Oberlander, designer of the creative playground at Montreal's Expo '67, and Paul Hogan, former U.S. International Year of the Child Commissioner. In England, observed Hogan, children were given opportunities "to play and grow, to work and invent, build and create, to be alone or seek help when needed." In North America, by contrast, children are given specific play equipment with detailed instructions on how to use it. "We spend ninety-five percent of our funds on concrete," says Hogan. "Even that wouldn't be so bad if we could ever finish what we start."

...in the adventure spirit

Which brings us to backyard adventure—the last (and maybe best) creative frontier for North American city and suburban kids. If they're not going to get adventure in parks, we've got to provide it at home. Here's an illustration of how it can be done:

Valerie Fronczek is director of the Children's Play Resources Center in Vancouver, B.C., a nonprofit organization, which (among other things) helps parents provide healthy play environments for their children at home. Widely respected as well for her work with the International Association for the Child's Right To Play, Fronczek's philosophy draws heavily from her own adventure-filled upbringing in England. Among friends and neighbors, however, she is much better known as the owner of the best backyard in town.

Bemoaning the fact that her two children might not get the same play opportunities in the local parks as she enjoyed in England, Fronczek decided to carve up her backyard into parents' and kids' sections and give each party absolute rights over their own territory—to make masterpieces, messes, and whatever fell in between. The children's 400-square-foot section started as a sand dump in the preschool years. With a handy supply of water and plenty of scooping, transporting and building

4

tools, the Fronczek children got into the habit of constructing fantasy cities. Within a few years they had progressed to wood, nails and scavenged materials.

Valerie routinely took them on rounds of the neighborhood's back alleys on garbage day, making stops at construction sites and garage sales along the way. They collected scrap wood, rope, tires, broken down tables, three-legged chairs, old roof shingles — all of which were eventually recycled into playhouses, canal systems, highways, bridges...you name it.

They were particularly adept at fort building. At one point, Valerie counted thirteen forts in the yard, most of them supported in trees, some perched atop a spy-out ramp that skirted the fence, allowing the young double-agents to surreptitiously monitor all comings and goings in the quiet suburban neighborhood. But they frequently broke out of hiding to paper the neighborhood with posters advertising impromptu puppet shows or gymnastic events to be staged in their own ramshackle amphitheater. The nickels and dimes they collected at the gate went toward a box of nails or a new augur bit.

Of course there were accidents, not only involving the young Fronczeks but their friends as well. Fingers were bashed by hammers, and ankles were sprained in falls from treehouses. But Valerie Fronczek never worried much about injuries, nor about her liability. In her mind there simply was no better way for children to grow up, hazards and all.

But that kind of confidence is premised on certain conditions. First of all, you must know your children and your neighbors' children well. They must be trustworthy; they must be mature enough physically to handle heights and hammers; they must have a degree of emotional maturity to handle the pressures of cooperative play. It is also crucial that they and their parents fully understand the risks involved.

Allowing such risks will be beyond the ability of many parents. Not all of us are as relaxed (some will say foolish) as Valerie Fronczek (whose son, incidentally, has gone on to a career in playground leadership). The important thing is to know your own anxiety level and plan accordingly.

If you can't bear the sound of a hammer banging away in the deep recesses of your yard, outlaw it. It is better to be clear about your tolerance (or lack of it) from the start than to invite your child to take a risk and then hover over him through every stage of the project. Adventure play is all about building confidence and competence. Parental intervention guarantees to nip both in the bud.

Even so, Valerie Fronczek never disappeared for long stretches of time while countless young builders banged and sawed away in her backyard. She was rarely out of sight, never out of earshot, and made a habit of patrolling the grounds each evening after the work crew was scrubbed, fed and safely tucked in. Flashlight and hammer in hand, she would stalk the fortresses, searching for loose rungs on ladders, groaning support beams, gaps in platforms and protruding nails. She closely supervised, without intervening.

...a complex compromise

The most appealing thing about adventure play for children is the level of complexity that it offers. Faced with the need to compromise (due to limited space, shaky nerves or whatever) it is certainly possible to offer your children a richly complex play experience short of Fronczek-style adventure.

In broad terms, a complex play experience is always more valuable than a simple one because it sustains interest on different levels. For example, an activity such as building a fort, which stimulates the child physically, cognitively and creatively, offers far greater rewards than riding a trike up and down the driveway — a basically physical activity. The professionals would say that fort-building has greater *play value* than trike-riding.

Ideally, a complex plaything stimulates the child to make her own decision about how to use it, or what to do with it, while the simple toy dictates use.

One easy measure of play value is the number of movable parts in a unit affording opportunities for children to manipulate and change elements in it. For example, a massive climbing structure with no moving parts has far less play value than a collection of sawhorses and walking boards that can be grouped and stacked to form a wide variety of different structures.

Likewise, a simple homemade scooter board (costs about $20, see page 64), which can be used to haul a load, to take teddy for a walk or to scoot about in any of a dozen body positions, has greater play value than a fixed riding toy on springs (costs up to $400, see page 44.)

You might assume play value would relate to the monetary value of a plaything. Fortunately, that isn't the rule, though too many well-intentioned parents measure play value by the price tag. If their children tire of an expensive toy after only a few minutes, parents often reprimand them for being wasteful or ungrateful.

Children are able to spend more concentrated periods of time in complex play environments because, though they do generally get bored with any single plaything, they never get bored with playing. It's a simple rule of thumb, but routinely overlooked by grown-ups who can't resist pretty toys.

An added pitfall to buying toys for the backyard is the temptation to make them blend with the petunias. You want your backyard to look attractive, so you buy attractive playthings — maybe a bright red locomotive that doubles as a picnic table. The problem arises when your children never have the opportunity to question what it is they are riding in. They are always conductors, passengers and engineers. Somehow it doesn't feel right to launch your bright red locomotive into space, or sail it across the high seas, or fill it with water and pretend it's the Titanic (anyway, Mommy would never approve). High aesthetics, low play value.

Simply built, nonrepresentational play equipment — preferably left with a natural wood stain or painted a single subdued color — can become whatever the child wants it to be for a day, an hour or just a minute. The barrel-and-cradle on

7

page 50 can be a space capsule to ride in, a horse to ride on or a tunnel to clamber through. The climbing frame on page 97 can be a two-story clubhouse, a fully furnished apartment building, a jungle gym or crow's nest lookout.

These playthings needn't look ugly, nor should they necessarily overshadow your prize shrubbery. Children like pretty things as much as their parents do — it's just that their sense of what's pretty is not normally accompanied by an adult's sense of strict order.

Of course, adults pay the bills, which is why commercial play equipment manufacturers go for the orderly look. They know the consumer will prefer the gym set with the least number of moving parts because it looks slick. Likewise, landscape architects know who foots the bills for their deck and garden renovations. It is no coincidence that design professionals so often favor suppliers like Denmark's Kompan Playscapes Inc., which produces sleek, exquisitely detailed playthings, including slides priced up to $2,000.

Still, you are better off buying designer toys than no toys at all. (And in fact, Kompan makes some wonderful equipment that I'd buy tomorrow if I won a lottery.) Naturalists may argue the point, but most play experts agree that open grassy spaces, however pastoral and charming to the adult eye, provide insufficient stimulation for ongoing play.

"Children need concrete, tangible things to manipulate," say Elizabeth Prescott and Sybil Kitchevsky in their "Physical Space" study for Washington's National Association for the Education of Young Children. "Botanical nature, in and of itself, does not seem sufficient to keep them interested on a daily basis."

(Prescott and Kitchevsky go on to suggest that while the adult mind is stimulated by brightly colored objects, the child's mind is actually distracted by color. Often a gaily colored object will fail to provide a "focus of activity" for children, while the same object, unpainted, will stimulate action as well as imagination.)

So, you can save a lot of money over the years by providing equipment that appeals to your children's play sense rather than your own design sense. A complex toy not only serves a variety of immediate uses, it more easily adapts to future uses as your children's developmental needs change.

Take slides, for example. A two-year-old will delight in the simple challenge of climbing up and sliding down. A three-year-old will want to go down in a variety of positions, none of them predictable. A four-year-old will try to run up the slide. A five-year-old will leap from the top and a six-year-old will walk right past with a blasé look on his face.

If you provide the growing child with a typical department store slide, you are asking for trouble. Those structures (the basic strip of sheet metal supported by a ladder) are designed for simply climbing up and sliding down. Unless you personally supervise the equipment, or issue a fully illustrated users' guide and rule book, you can count on the thing being abused in all the above variations. Only the two-year-old is using the slide in the manner for which it was built. Only she is

safe — that is, if a two-year-old can be considered safe anywhere but asleep in bed.

Give your kids a well designed, wide-bodied slide, on the other hand, and everyone will be satisfied. The two-year-old is safer, because the well designed slide (unlike the department store variety) takes off from a platform that is roomy enough to accommodate her footwork as she switches from climbing to sitting position. The three-year-old can safely spin, roll, shimmy and twist down the wide slide without going off an edge. The four- and five-year-olds benefit from the wide slide's increased stability, and the six-year-old may find renewed interest in sliding as a social event — let's see how many of us can slide down together if we link arms.

Make that slide a detachable component of your play structure, and even older children will enjoy repositioning it at different levels, or finding their own revolutionary methods of sliding.

Once you start thinking *complex*, you will naturally make the right decisions for your family. You will seriously consider a tire swing over the conventional type when you realize the play value inherent in a rig that allows safe multidirectional swinging, a choice of position (standing, sitting or lying down) plus the social value of teaming two or three swingers together around the rim. Likewise, a sandbox designed for parallel water play is more complex than the usual dry variety — and all it takes to make the difference is a drain hole, a "cake table" to work on (see page 127) and a hose nearby.

In short, complexity invites the child to manipulate and alter things, for his own benefit and for yours. Ask any experienced school teacher how the right choice of

9

play equipment affects children's lives. Complexity promotes extended play with a single unit, rather than the kind of distracted cruising from unit to unit that is typically observed in children who are surrounded by poorly designed toys. Children will spend greater periods of time with fewer pieces of equipment — which can save money as well as yard space.

Complex toys can also save a lot of aggravation over conflicts in the play area. Single-use toys are difficult to share. The more options you present to the children, the less they will argue over how a toy is "supposed" to be used, who uses it best, who gets to use it first, or who's next in line.

What Adults Need To Do To Let Children Play

Do you relish the thought of opening your back door after breakfast and watching a brightly colored blur of children disappear through it — into their own engrossing world of play?

The first stage on the road to independence may, in fact, seem like backpeddling. You must involve yourself deeply in the process of backyard planning along with your children. The method I've adopted (with due credit to Dr. Alfred Dreykurs) is called the family council.

It may seem a lot easier to make unilateral decisions — to arrive home one day, Santa Claus-like, with a complete snap-together backyard in the trunk of your car. But alas, you'll soon discover you've spent the entire backyard budget, the whole lawn is used up, and the kids still don't have the playhouse they really wanted in the first place.

A treehouse that dreams are made of, drawn by Anna Slade, age 8.

10

The family council is such a basic planning and conflict-solving tool that once you start the ball rolling, you will doubtless find you are convening it for all kinds of other family matters. Here is how the system might work:

1. Post an agenda on the refrigerator at least a day before the meeting, outlining the issues up for discussion. That way everyone knows what's to be decided, and no one can complain later about not being heard. (Don't leave the little tots in the dark. Make it clear to them what's happening, and how they can contribute — for example, by drawing a picture of the house and yard.)

2. Set meeting times carefully so everyone can be there, and so no one will be rushing off to other activities or nodding off to sleep.

3. The first meeting should aim for consensus in a very general way: Record what each member would like to see in the yard. Discuss ways of incorporating various elements and of keeping expectations in line with budget. Take a close look at the family's indoor–outdoor activity patterns and the climate in your region. Does it make sense to build permanent outdoor structures for year-round play or to use smaller freestanding equipment, which can be carried inside for play during the winter?

4. Assign duties. In the initial stages, concentrate on data: Mom might be in charge of drawing up a budget; Dad might start poking around the local lumberyard; one child might be sent around the block, while another is posted to nearby parks and playgrounds to survey the already existing play opportunities in the neighborhood.

If space is limited in your yard, you may decide to drop swings from your plan. After all, most playgrounds have them, so their absence at home will only make your regular playground visits that much more fun. Remember, your yard is not a prison. No matter how much fun they can have at home, the kids will still visit their friends' houses and trek to the park. Why duplicate pleasures?

Likewise, refrain from keeping up with the Joneses. Not everyone on the block needs a 6-foot square sandbox. Why not offer the neighborhood children something different from what's in their own backyards? They'll clamber to play with your kids, and everyone will win.

5. All family members should be encouraged to take pen to paper, especially in the early stages, making lists or sketching backyard scenarios both real and imagined. This is particularly valuable for very young children. Ask a three-year-old what he likes playing with the most and he may struggle to find an answer. But let him draw his fantasy playhouse and you're getting somewhere. (Don't throw these masterpieces away. In fact don't throw the surveys and lists away either. It is amusing and often extremely valuable to measure the end product against the original intentions.)

6. Continue the assignment process indefinitely. During construction you will need supervisors, builders, helpers, snack fetchers…and once it's complete, there is regular maintenance, safety checks and clean-up. It is a good idea to post these

duties, so everyone knows without asking (or arguing) what his job is.

7. Call the council only when absolutely necessary. In the start-up stage you may require a couple of back-to-back meetings to allow researchers to bring information forward. But once the project is moving along, with tasks defined and rules clearly spelled out, the council should go into fairly lengthy periods of recess. Otherwise, plans can be derailed over a whim; and time and money can be wasted if the family council process takes precedence over the physical work.

On the other hand, be aware of developing conflicts. Keep the plan flexible enough so that it can be derailed when necessary — perhaps redefined or redrawn — to take in some important new observation or desire that couldn't be anticipated at the outset. After all, the point of this process is to promote a truly cooperative effort in your yard and to allow for staged construction. You may need to test an idea. It may fail, and you'll have to return to the drawing boards. Nothing ventured, nothing gained.

Don't shy away from the family council idea if it sounds too formal for your tastes. There is no reason why the planning process can't take place across the dinner table, readjourned around the evening bath, or even during a break from a bedtime story.

Planning to avoid conflict

A very important goal of careful planning should be the elimination (or at least limitation) of conflict *at* play. Battles will occur now and then, naturally. But it is crucial to keep the conflicts and the conflict-solving discussions as far from the play area as possible. Otherwise you will find yourself constantly dragged in to act as referee, to judge who is out of line, who is being a bully, and why the little guy keeps getting hurt.

By following a democratic process, most conflicts will be dealt with before they become obstacles to the enjoyment of your yard. Conflicts will be settled between people rather than aggravated by the yard's design, which is a sad but extremely common state of affairs.

...see you later

With the decision-making process in place and the play area shaping up nicely, you are now ready to face the greatest challenge of all — extricating yourself from the action. To do so, you must be truly prepared to back out gracefully. Lots of parents pay lip service to it, but few are willing and able to seriously let out the leash.

The professionals tell us that if we can learn to trust our children, then they will very quickly become trustworthy. But it's not always an easy lesson. Of course, the whole notion of independence really comes to bear only after the first three years, and even then, you can expect a somewhat hazardous transition. But if you can get a

grip on your nerves and somehow manage to observe at a safe distance without constantly intervening, then you will find that you pass through the danger zone with
far less mishap then you ever believed possible.

While there is no firm rule about the age of autonomy, children younger than
three usually require constant hands-on supervision. This is not only because they
are accident-prone, but because most toddlers have trouble accepting their mother's
or caretaker's absence from sight for longer than a few minutes at a time. After age
three, most children will play happily on their own for short periods of time, as long
as they know clearly where their caretaker is so that contact can be resumed at very
short notice.

The kind of protecting–retrieving systems required for very young children
come naturally to most parents. Allowing a child to explore does not mean supress-
ing those instincts. "Together the child and the caretaker work as a learning system
to experiment with and evaluate the child's ability to explore new places and situa-
tions without serious physical danger," explain American researchers Cecilia Perez
and Roger A. Hart.

Beyond the age of three, a leap of faith is required on both sides. Naturally,
some parents have more faith in their children's abilities than do others. Not all of us
are prepared to go as far as Valerie Fronczek did in allowing her children to take
measured risks. Some parents feel content taking one step at a time in that direction,
acknowledging that risk is at the very heart of play. Children will naturally take
risks, whether we condone it or not. The decision we must make for ourselves is
how close to hover and how much to let go.

The cost of liability makes it very difficult for public officials to condone any
degree of risk-taking in parks and playgrounds. One such official confided to me his
deep sadness that the rising cost of public insurance and the attendant paranoia
about accidents is going to force all the really fun pieces of play equipment into ex-
tinction—starting with swings, seesaws and cable rides. And the same will go for
playhouses with roofs (from which children can take falls) and solid walls (that
obscure the view of supervisors) because recent injunctions have forced school
boards to ban these playthings.

The folly of all this is that it forces children to go out and take risks in inap-
propriate places, such as real rooftops and busy streets, because without risks, there
is no growth. "Serious restriction of exploration will deny a child the ability to
develop into a competent, happy individual and is to be avoided at all costs," write
Perez and Hart.

If this developmental need is acknowledged and provisions are made for
relatively safe risk-taking, children will quickly learn to gauge their challenges
realistically, setting each new goal just a little beyond their current grasp. If adults
attempt to block the process, the child's frustration may prevent levelheaded
judgements, making accidents much more likely to happen.

CHAPTER 2

The Ground Rules

Your backyard is not a public playground, and that is a distinct advantage. You don't have to design for heavy play traffic on your equipment. You are not obliged to make your yard as safe as a padded cell in order to avoid injury claims at all costs. You don't have the civic child care authorities breathing down your neck, enforcing their design guidelines to ensure that your yard offers a perfect balance of motor, social and creative play opportunities.

So you have a lot of freedom. But you also have an enormous responsibility to your own children and their friends. You have a choice: You can study the field, incorporating the best public playground features into your yard—the proper surface materials, foundation timbers and retaining structures, the safety measures and codes of conduct—tailoring all of these, naturally, to fit your space and budget; or you can wing it, and lie awake nights wondering if you've done the right thing.

Now that you're with me, let's take a hard look at how the professionals design for play.

Please, fall here

Accidents involving swings, slides and climbers account for almost one-fifth of all hospital-treated injuries to North American children between the ages of two and nine years. Most of the serious injuries are a direct result of contact with inadequate impact surface under the play equipment—in other words, from falls onto grass, packed earth or worse.

This is a tough issue to face in backyard play. Very few families even consider the impact surface under their swing sets. After all, kids have been swinging,

15

dangling and climbing over plain, unadorned dirt for centuries. Just because public playground planners are getting hysterical about injury claims, why should we follow suit?

Let me speak from experience. I stewed over the prospect of installing impact surface in my yard for more than a year, postponing plans for the play structure that we all wanted to build. The very idea of putting in a 200-square-foot retaining structure, trucking in four tons of impact sand and then spending my weekends raking out the pet droppings gave me one long anxiety attack. At one point I was prepared to forget the whole idea of installing play equipment. It seemed far too complicated, and too costly.

I changed my mind, looking ahead to a four- or five-year payoff on a relatively moderate investment. We bowed to the safety factor, put some climbing equipment on a proper bed of sand, and the kids were in business for under $300 and a few days' labor. But if you maintain that it's not worth the price or bother, you are probably right—for your own family. If you can't afford safe surfacing, you really can't afford that three-level climber with the 15-foot fireman's pole and 12-foot slide. Let your kids play safely on tall structures in properly designed public playgrounds. Don't take the risk at home.

As a general rule, grass and packed earth provide inadequate cushioning wherever a child may fall from a height of 30 inches or more. If your children are older than four and have the cat-like ability to land lightly on their feet, you may be able to stretch that limit to 40 inches. Beyond that, a child may sustain a concussion or worse. You are better off providing "low-altitude" play experiences in your yard—sand and water, arts and crafts, playhouse construction, riding toys and the like—if you are unable to provide adequate ground surfacing for "high altitude" play.

But if you decide to go the distance at home, there's a bonus in it for your kids. The sand or pea gravel you use to surface the play area will be quite different from the stuff in the sandbox, giving them a whole new dimension of creative play. It is generally coarser stuff—not great for building, but ideal for transporting in dump-trucks, shovelling into great heaps, or supporting miniature forests, battle flags and tepees.

The use of proper surfacing also enables your children to stretch themselves to the limits of the equipment, to take greater risks and reap greater enjoyment. This is especially true for the very young, who can easily be turned off the whole climb-ing–swinging–tumbling experience by a single painful fall.

This is true not only for tall climbers but for low-slung gym equipment as well. It is pointless to install a wooden vault or parallel bars over a hard surface (packed dirt and grass are only marginally softer than asphalt, see chart page 17). Kids aren't fools. You can count on them to master only the safest exercises under such risky conditions.

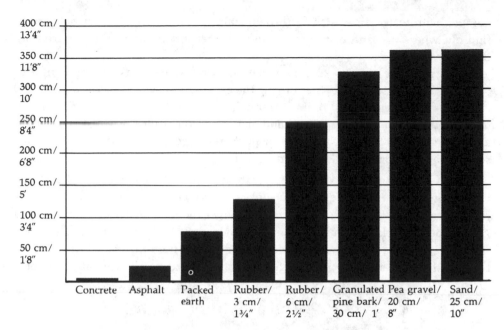

| 400 cm/ 13'4" |
| 350 cm/ 11'8" |
| 300 cm/ 10' |
| 250 cm/ 8'4" |
| 200 cm/ 6'8" |
| 150 cm/ 5' |
| 100 cm/ 3'4" |
| 50 cm/ 1'8" |

Concrete Asphalt Packed earth Rubber/ 3 cm/ 1¾" Rubber/ 6 cm/ 2½" Granulated pine bark/ 30 cm/ 1' 8" Pea gravel/ 20 cm/ 8" Sand/ 25 cm/ 10"

Table shows the height from which a child can fall head-first onto different surfaces before the critical limit for causing concussion, expressed as 50 G, is exceeded.

Reprinted with permission from The Franklin Institute Research Laboratories, U.S.A.

...sand and other soft stuff

Your choice of surfacing will be affected by the natural resources of your area as well as by your budget. You may choose river sand if access is easy, or bark chips if forest industry by-products are available. There are also aesthetic considerations.

Sand: Fill to a depth of at least 10 inches using round-particle sand to minimize packing. In most regions washed river sand is ideal and surprisingly inexpensive (about $12 a cubic yard in our neck of the woods). But beware of high clay content, which will cause river sand to pack.

Wind-blown sand of the type found in dunes is also ideal because of the uniform particle size—they move easily against each other on impact, yielding instantly as the child lands. Unfortunately this fine sand will treat your yard like a dune, so don't use it without first planting shrubs or landscaping mounds to break the wind.

Sand and gravel companies will generally truck washed construction sand into your yard for a nominal delivery charge. (You can also buy it in hundred-pound bags, if you prefer, and drag it home yourself. Just be warned: An average backyard climber should sit on a couple of tons.) Call around to find a company with good rates on small orders. When it arrives, make sure it is adequately washed before accepting the load: Scoop a small amount of the sand onto a light-colored cloth,

17

dampen with water and watch for brown staining. Also make it your business to find out where the sand comes from, and whether it contains pollutants from industry or agriculture.

You won't be able to keep your surface sand as clean as the stuff in your covered sandbox, so don't bother buying the expensive sterilized sand. Impact sand is chiefly for landing on and running through, not for cake making. As long as toddlers are discouraged from regular hand play in it, you needn't be overly concerned about hygiene. Patrol the area with a pooper-scooper when necessary; rake for smooth landings and a well groomed appearance.

Pea Gravel: You'll need a little less of this to afford the same degree of cushioning—about 8 inches is adequate. But unless you've got a sturdy pickup truck or heavy-suspension jeep, you should definitely get the stuff delivered. Because pea gravel doesn't pack like sand, it actually provides superior cushioning. The down side becomes apparent, however, when a child lands nose-first in a heap of these tough little pebbles. It may be tops at preventing major breaks and sprains, but it

sure can scrape and scratch! Visit a sand and gravel contractor before placing your order. There are various grades available, and if you choose carefully, you can avoid years of skinned knees and torn jeans. Look for rounded, well washed particles (unwashed pea gravel is very dirty stuff to play in).

Bark Chips: It goes by different names in different areas, but the basic ingredient is granulated tree bark. Fir is best, pine is acceptable, but cedar is definitely a problem because of splinters. In general, look for rounded nuggets of medium size (small nuggets decompose too quickly; large ones can be abrasive).

Some people prefer bark to sand or gravel because it is lightweight, relatively inexpensive, and looks attractive, especially at the base of a naturally finished wood structure. Unfortunately, you'll need an awful lot of it — one foot deep for adequate impact value — and at that depth it is very difficult to keep it clear of animal droppings, insects, bubble gum and dozens of other things. Also, once wet, it is very difficult to dry because of the bulk, so you can expect rapid decomposition in rainy climates. Even in drier areas it may need to be replaced once a year.

In dry, windy locations bark chips can create a dust problem. In any location, chips easily adhere to running shoe treads and become a regular feature on hall and kitchen floors. One solution to most of these problems is to cover the mulch with a tarp of oilcloth or indoor–outdoor carpeting. The tarp can be secured at the corners, or simply tucked in around the retaining walls, and periodically shaken or swept off.

Mixtures: It takes more effort to cart it in from various suppliers, but many professionals prefer combinations of pea gravel and sand, or pea gravel and chips, to the single surface material. The gravel keeps the sand from packing, while leaving play value intact; and gravel mixed with bark keeps the chips down, without diminishing the cushioning effect.

Rubber: Most of us cannot even consider a rubber fall surface because only the thickest grades are safe enough (2½ inches and up), and those are wildly expensive in large quantities. If you're resourceful, however, you may be able to scavenge used gym mats from schools or other community facilities. These are especially suitable for indoor play areas.

Grass: Grass invites accidents because it looks much softer than it is. It cannot stand up to the varied abuses your average tumbler will inflict. Grass will soon wear down to dirt, which neither looks soft nor is soft. You will find yourself moving the jungle gym or slide to different parts of the yard, leaving a trail of dirt patches, which never seem to resprout. Drainage can also be a problem.

...keeping it all together

Whether you choose sand, pea gravel, bark chips or a mixture, you will need a retaining structure to keep it all in place. Partially sunken timbers are best in backyards (concrete retainers are too much bother and too permanent for most

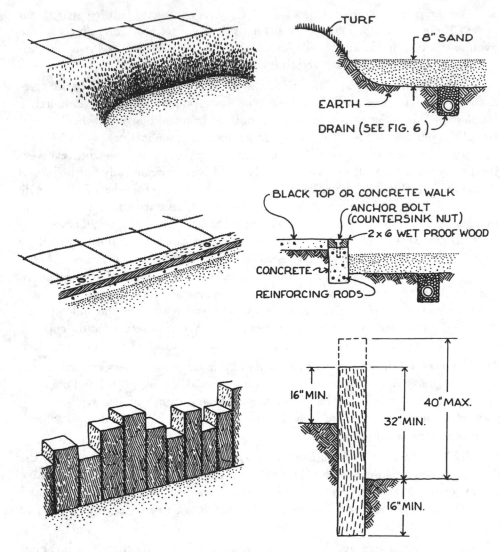

TURF

8" SAND

EARTH

DRAIN (SEE FIG. 6)

BLACK TOP OR CONCRETE WALK

ANCHOR BOLT
(COUNTERSINK NUT)

2 x 6 WET PROOF WOOD

CONCRETE

REINFORCING RODS

16" MIN.

40" MAX.

32" MIN.

16" MIN.

Ground cover retainers: (top to bottom), natural turf, concrete, and partially sunken timbers

Reprinted with permission from *How To Make Your
Backyard More Interesting Than TV*
by Jay Beckwith, McGraw-Hill Book Co., 1980

families, while core logs are too expensive). Sink the timbers at least 8 inches into the ground, allowing for 8 to 12 inches of cover, and another 4 to 6 inches of wood to protrude.

Redwood and cedar retainers are the best choices because of their natural resistance to decay. Even so, wood in contact with the ground must be chemically preserved. Lumber yards will supply you with appropriately pretreated lumber (be sure to specify nontoxic, for playground use). If you are doing your own cutting, you will need extra sealant for the cut edges because most commercial treatment does not penetrate through to the core. Be sure to keep children away from all wood preservatives until dry. There is debate over the safeness of even the nontoxic varieties.

Avoid using recycled telephone poles or railway ties, as creosote sealants may weep in the warm sun, releasing toxic oils. There is no debate about the lethal qualitites of creosote. Keep it out of the play area, except when applied (cautiously) to the deeply sunken portion of support poles. (See detail opposite page.)

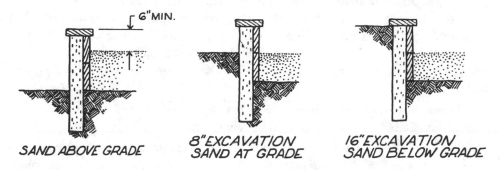

SAND ABOVE GRADE   8"EXCAVATION   16"EXCAVATION
                         SAND AT GRADE   SAND BELOW GRADE

Reprinted with permission from *How To Make Your
Backyard More Interesting Than TV*
by Jay Beckwith, McGraw-Hill Book Co., 1980

In rainy areas, keep the ground cover above grade. Drainage can be a serious problem if you excavate, unless you run a leach pipe under the cover material.

Study the play equipment to determine the area required to cover. If you are buying a climbing–gym unit, the manufacturer will specify the surface area required for ground cover. If you are building your own, be sure to include generous safety margins in every direction. As a general rule for climbing equipment, leave one foot of empty impact surface (in all directions) for each foot of height. For example, an 8-foot climber needs 8 feet of surface in each direction—enough for safe leaping and falling from every possible angle. Swings require at least 6 feet beyond the outer limit of the swinging arc. Provide at least 4 square feet for slide landings. (More details on safe swings and slides in Chapter 6.)

These margins are important not only to provide a cushion where needed, but to ensure that the retainer itself does not present a hazard. Statistics show that almost as many lower leg and head injuries result from striking wood or concrete retainers as from falling straight onto hard ground.

Rules of the Game

As in all areas of discipline with children, rules are a necessary precondition to freedom. Only with a clear understanding of limits can children securely test themselves, break new ground and eventually set their own reasonable limits. All this is doubly important outdoors where many of the physical limits and boundaries of "the acceptable" are not evident. Even so, the rules of fair and safe play must be evident — both for the children's benefit and for the parents' peace of mind.

The following is a suggested rule list only. Your own rules will relate to the age, ability and number of children who normally play in your yard, plus the degree of physical risk you are willing to live with. And remember, just as important as the rule list is your determined effort to apply it consistently.

Tools: Follow a strict take-out and put-away code. Only a certain number of tools should be taken out at one time. Only certain people should be authorized to take out, while others may be allowed to use specified tools as long as an older child or parent is on hand. It is a good idea to organize the storage area with your rules in mind, placing out-of-bound tools out of reach. Keep a first-aid kit handy in case of accidents.

Dress code: Avoid large hoods, loose scarves, capes or anything that could get caught on climbing, swinging and sliding equipment.

Supervision: If an adult is not available for hands-on supervision of construction activities or risky physical play, appoint a responsible older child to supervise. This should be a rotating job, to prevent overburdening one child.

Liability: Make sure all visitors to the yard "check in" with the supervisor before joining in. Make sure visitors' parents understand any potential risks (get their consent in writing if you are nervous). While these steps will not necessarily limit your liability, they will alert you to children's comings and goings. You should know the limits of your homeowner's liability insurance.

Clean-up: All participants should help put toys and loose equipment back into storage after use. Rather than singling out offenders (a practice that inevitably leads to long-winded debates over whose mess is whose, who cleaned up yesterday, who cleans up fast and who pokes around), make it a policy to apply punishment across the board. If everyone is responsible for putting away, children will have to work it out on their own.

Inspection: Ultimately you are responsible for the safety of the play equipment in your yard. No matter what you build or buy, it must be checked periodically to ensure that:

    — all cracked, warped or rusted pieces of climbing equipment are replaced
    — moving parts move freely
    — bearings are oiled
    — all concrete footings are at least 6 inches below grade
    — there is no wood rot
    — edges of wood and metal are smooth
    — all fastenings, handrails, ladder rungs and steps are secure

Pay special attention to any play structures built by children or by well-meaning but poorly informed adults. *A child can suffer strangulation or a broken neck if a climber, ladder or ramp has a gap of between 4 and 9 inches wide.* (More details on home-built safety in Chapter 5.)

The family council is an ideal vehicle for rule setting, especially when it comes to the safe limits of physical play (one of the hardest areas in which to win cooperation). When the children are part of the decision-making process, they are much more inclined to live with the decisions. At a recent meeting in Cincinnati, Ohio, of the International Association for the Child's Right to Play, the following list of rules was presented by a group of children for safe play in their own playground:

— Don't jump out of high swings.
— Swing properly; no bumpers, twists, flips, dives, climbs or doublerides.
— Don't slide head first.
— Don't walk up or down the slide.
— Don't run with anything in your mouth (except your braces).

A sunken design allows quick clean-up with a broom.

A Place for Everything

A proper storage system is one of the most valuable assets of a well designed play area, however large or small. Unfortunately, most of us realize the importance of a storage sytem only after we've allowed the deck or driveway to randomly (and often dangerously) collect layer upon layer of stuff. Without an orderly system of putting things away, things will not be put away. Seems obvious, doesn't it? But even so, we tend to apply such rules only indoors, and soon even those items that survive the human and climatic ravages somehow lose their play value—just because they've been sitting around too long in front of everyone's nose.

Whether you are designing an entire play yard or enhancing a terrace, deck or patio, it pays to treat storage as a basic necessity and to design it in. You can run into difficulties if you expect the garden shed to double as play storage. For one thing, you must create a physical barrier between hedge clippers and sand toys if there are young children about. Also, your all-purpose shed should be suitably located within easy reach of the primary play areas as well as the garden.

The same considerations apply to the use of garage space for storage—a very common system that is in most cases seriously flawed. Garages tend to be off the beaten play path, with the result that trikes and wagons get dumped there by an irate parent at the end of the day, rather than driven in and out during the course of play.

To get maximum use of a toy storage unit, plan a separate structure that is in scale with its primary users (the children) and is easily accessible to them. A shallow, low-slung cabinet bordering one fence, perhaps under the porch or attached to the deck, is ideal for youngsters because it is sufficiently handy to make the constant "taking out" and "putting back" a natural part of their play experience. If the task is too difficult or awkward, then you can't expect children to *want* to do it.

The storage area should have a modular design, easily adaptable to changes in toys and equipment as the kids grow. A roomy area for push toys and trikes has to eventually accommodate two-wheelers and field hockey gear. And shelf space designed to hold size two shoe boxes filled with your toddler's chalk and play-dough should expand to hold size eight shoe boxes filled with rock collections.

Playground leaders and teachers have long understood the value of well-ordered storage. Things which have to be taken from a closed (preferably locked) cabinet have a special attraction to children of all ages. Giving the child access to the cabinet, via his own key, increases the intrigue and invariably increases his sense of responsibility for the cabinet's contents. (It is well documented in child behavior studies that the more objects are removed from a child's reach, the more destructive he becomes.)

Using storage is therefore not merely a question of removing and retrieving things, but a method of organization that can greatly enhance a child's sense of his own possessions—his pride in them and his interest in their use.

Organized storage also increases the complexity of an activity and, correspondingly, the time spent in play. Taking objects out of storage gives the child a view of what else might be taken out later, spurring future game plans, and sparking initiative and imagination.

CHAPTER 3

Making The Most Of It

I f we all lived on gently rolling quarter-acre lots in neatly carved subdivisions, play area design would present very little challenge. It would simply be a matter of finding a sheltered corner for sand and water play, a screened area for fort-building (and other messy pastimes), some wide-open space for gross motor play and a spot on the patio for quiet-time projects.

But our cities and suburban areas are far more diverse than that, making our design challenges far greater. Try squeezing the same range of activities onto a 33-foot lot, or a hillside lot, or a densely wooded one. Try squeezing *anything* into the play space provided in a standard city apartment, for that matter.

There is one solution that will work for many of these problems. It's called "loose parts" — an increasingly common catchphrase used by playground designers who see it as a perfect companion to the "complex play" philosophy. Loose parts are relatively small, movable pieces of play equipment that lend themselves to a wide variety of uses, depending on the lay of the land and the whims of the children at play. With an efficient storage system in place, components can be taken out a few at a time for play in small areas. They can likewise be carried indoors during inclement weather.

A typical collection of loose parts would contain some combination of the following:

— A-frames of various sizes and strengths to be climbed on or used as supports in larger play structures;
— cleated boards for walking on, leaping from or stacking into skyscrapers;
— oversized hollow or notched blocks for building;
— stepladders for access;
— horizontal ladders placed high for feats of strength or low for balance;
— tires to bounce on, swing in and climb through;

— ropes for lashing, dangling, hand-over-hand climbing or tightrope walking;
— things that rock for seafaring;
— things that roll for hauling loads.

The developmental advantage of loose elements (sometimes called "constructive" elements) in a play area is that children can manipulate and radically rearrange them as they go. They can play with them on many levels, challenging themselves physically, inventing games and living out new fantasies daily.

Take loose parts to the limit, and you end up with a full-fledged adventure playground (basically a child-scale construction site). Most kids would think they'd arrived at heaven's gate if they woke up one morning to find a heap of scrap lumber, rope, barrels, tires and cable spools waiting for them outside the kitchen door, with a cheerful parent standing by to dole out the hammer, nails and Band-Aids.

But you needn't take it to such adventurous limits. Just start out with a modest collection, tailored to your personal space and ability to live with the clutter. (For details on buying, scavenging and building your own loose parts, turn to chapters 4 and 5.)

Rocks and Rolls

If the uneven lay of your land makes it difficult to install traditional play equipment, do not despair. And do not (by any means) call in the bulldozers. Consider yourself lucky. You can do far more with natural slopes, mounds and rock outcroppings than most people dream of doing on their pancake-flat lawns. In fact, you can get away with installing much less for your children by taking advantage of the built-in sliding, rolling and hiding potential of your yard.

If, for example, you have a natural vale, run a leach pipe through and fill it with sand. Add a climbing frame or some gym equipment and you have a natural tumbling area. If you live in a rainy area (and if you happen to have a mud room on your porch where the kids can strip down and shake off before reentering civilization) you will get maximum play value out of those little gullies by just leaving them to collect water. For more on wet delights, see page 129.

The very best piece of play equipment in the world is a hill. If every child had one or two hills (they don't need to be very big) the people who sell climbers would be out of business. Elevational change is a natural high of childhood—not only getting up there but running, rolling, sliding, biking or tobogganing down. And hills are not hard to make, yet few of us bother. All it takes is a load of earth and some grass seed.

In the backyard scale of things, hills should really be called mounds. The best slope ratio for mound playing is 1:3 (in other words for every one unit of vertical rise, allow three units of horizontal run). This ratio best provides sufficient downhill momentum, while preventing erosion and allowing for easy mowing in the summer.

Mounds are also useful as shelter against prevailing winds. They can be grouped to create interior space for creative–social play (perhaps go for small, steeper mounds for this purpose—about 1:2 ratio). You can increase play value by building tunnels or slides into the slope, or by adding stepping logs or stones for climbing.

...and other natural advantages

Trees and shrubs provide similar play interest, as well as the obvious aesthetic advantages. In fact, they provide the natural solution to the main conflict of interest in backyards: While kids want their yard to be fun, parents want it to look pretty. The conflict intensifies after age six or seven when "fun" can entail building plywood shantytowns or burying treasure chests. Plants provide the compromise—let the kids make their mess—behind a screen of hawthorn.

A wooded yard also offers natural hideaways, activity barriers and windbreaks. If you haven't inherited trees or shrubs from previous owners, you now have the luxury of planting exactly the type you want, where you want them. If, on the

other hand, your back door leads into a small forest, you may want to clear away some of the foliage to provide more play space.

If you are planting, price need not be a serious deterrent. Buy small but fast-growing plants. Or scavenge along the highway's edge or a rural back road for wayward seedlings — little orphan trees that will be mowed down if you don't adopt them into your yard. (When in the transplanting mood, it is a good idea to carry a garden spade and some old pots in your trunk so you're always ready for action.) Just be sure not to tamper with seedling groves, or anything cultivated for that matter.

When planting shrubs, make the distinction between those to be used as barriers around the yard and those used for shelter or for playing under. The following grow into a bushy canopy just a foot or two above the ground (a little pruning will be necessary) and are therefore ideal to play under:

— Melaleuca, particularly armillaris, linarifolia and wilsonii*
— most species of Tamarisk*

- Salix (most willows)
- Photinia
- Cupressus (cypress)
- Syringa vulgaris (lilac)
- Vibernum tomentosum

The following are better suited for barriers, screens, enclosures for quiet corners and windbreaks:

- Abutilon (flowering maple)*
- Cortaderia (pampas grass)
- Mahonia (Oregon grape)
- Crataegus (hawthorn)
- Plumbago*
- bamboo

*Best suited to warm, dry climates, such as California.

Some of the loveliest landscaping plants are poisonous to children. Azalea, Hydrangea, Oleander and Rhododendron are just a few whose leaves, flowers or berries can pose a serious threat to naturally curious toddlers. Even a common vegetable garden can pose serious health risks—rhubarb leaves, tomato stems and potato sprouts are poisonous.

So plant with care. Consult with landscaping experts before choosing new varieties for your yard; similarly check out all existing plants, and be prepared to remove any that pose a threat. Of course, if you love plants you will not be able to remove all the poisonous varieties without stripping your garden bare. Just be sure the offending varieties are away from the play area, and that the children know clearly where they are and why they should not touch them.

For a more comprehensive list of poisonous plants, see Appendix II, page 173.

Small Spaces

In all play areas, large or small, equipment that can be broken down and put back together again (by little hands) is preferable to the permanently bolted or molded types. When working with limited space, however, necessity often outweighs personal preference. Being aware of this problem of limited space, a few manufacturers have brought out modular build-your-own gyms and oversized block sets that look like giant Konnectos or Legos. While traditionalists may have trouble tearing themselves away from wooden building blocks, they will have to concede to the tremendous advantages of lightweight plastics in this area. It's common to get some twenty or thirty component parts in a kit, and if space is at a premium, you're not going to be able to leave them lying around the play area from one day to the next. Plastics infinitely lighten the task of lugging them in and out of storage.

The sets with highest play value come with a wide variety of add-ons, including wheels, wall panels and ramps. Little Tikes has their "Activity Gym," Learning Products, Inc. has "Snap Land" and various major suppliers carry the wonderfully versatile "Quadro"—an all-in-one jungle gym, tunnel maze, puppet theater, playhouse, table-and-chairs set, airplane, go-cart and locomotive. (Galt has something similar, called Gymbo.) You can spend one hundred to one thousand dollars on these toys, depending on your ambitions and additions.

Buying a set can be an expensive way to fill the play area with loose parts. A less costly strategy is to buy bits and pieces as you come across them. Below are a few standard designs that lend themselves to compact spaces.

Cube Chairs: Made of wood or formed plastic, with a different seat height depending on which end is up, these little chairs are incredibly handy indoors and

More than a chair, the cube design offers a dozen creative possibilities beyond merely sitting.

The versatile rocking boat overturns to make a toddler slide.

out. The more you have the better. Double them up, one tipped in the low-seat position and the other in the high-seat position, to create a chair and table combo. Or use them simply as building blocks for towers, or as supports for lightweight boards.

Rocking Boat: Commonly available in wood or plastic, this rider–climber comes in small and large sizes to accommodate two or more children. Overturned, the small model becomes a set of steps with a platform on top (build it yourself, page 63). Many of the larger models reverse to form steps and a slide. Be sure to get the large type in a lightweight plastic so the children will be able to move it around or tip it over themselves for use in constructive play.

Junior Trampoline: The best models have removable handrails for little bouncers. Even so, use your trampoline with caution. Think about where to place it — ideally on a mat or other suitable impact surface, away from structures or access routes.

Sand and Water Play: This is one of the most creative and sustaining aspects of backyard play, especially for children younger than six. It would be a shame for your kids to miss out on it just because of space limitations. So consider doing what most daycare centers and preschools do—set up a sand and water station.

The most basic sand–water table is simple to improvise at home, with plastic basins on a movable table or workbench (get lockable casters). If you can spare the table, cut holes in the surface and sink the basins into it snugly. If you have a very restricted play area or terrace, keep basins small to prevent back strain when lugging the thing to and from the kitchen sink. If you have a patio with a water outlet and drain, go for a larger size with a tap and plug.

For variety in water play, add a drop or two of food coloring, soap flakes and a steady supply of household utensils, such as containers, funnels, sponges, sieves, or even ping-pong balls. For an afternoon's diversion, have your kids clean and repaint an exterior wall—with water and no food coloring, that is.

Ideal for patios and decks, a small sand table with drain can be a lot more fun than a great big, dry sandbox.

You can easily frame your own sand table, scaled to the available play space and to your children's reach. Nontoxic pressure-treated timbers are most durable, or you can finish raw wood with a few coats of marine enamel or spar varnish. (Regular exterior paints and urethane finishes aren't nearly as tough.)

Mixed sand and water play will have to be limited in small areas where lack of drainage and sunshine can lead to a chronically waterlogged box. If drainage is available, but sunshine is limited, first condition the inside of the box with three or four coats of fiberglass resin and drill a 3/4-inch drain hole in the bottom. Keep it plugged with a cork until draining time.

A Question of Balance

When planning for small or unusual spaces, the biggest challenge is reaching a balance in the kind of play opportunities offered. You can't give your kids everything they want (nor should you, regardless of lot size). But you should endeavor to give them the best possible mix of activities to provide maximum interest and stimulation under the circumstances.

Following is a list of the four essential types of play:

Motor: Children need tall things to climb, leap and swing from; they need moving things to ride, heavy things to lift, narrow things to balance on and round things to throw.

Social: Children need private places to plot rebellion, empty spaces for a game of marbles or tag, a table for tea parties.

Creative-Cognitive: Children need permission to build and destroy, preferably with messy materials such as sand, water, paints and clay. Blocks and other "clean" materials can be fun too.

Quiet: Children need a place they can retreat to, privately or in groups. It can be a lone swing, a sheltered spot near a tree or a hammock on the porch.

It may be clearly impossible for you to meet a number of these needs. That's okay, as long as your children are getting that stimulation elsewhere. Kids who grow up in apartments learn at an early age to burn off steam in the schoolyard, or at a neighborhood park. Likewise, kids who can't find a private retreat in a wide-open yard can always disappear into their bedrooms.

It is not necessary to separate the four dimensions by physical boundaries. In fact, even if you live on an acreage, you'd be wise to contain the play within one well-defined area and to run some of the activity "stations" together. In this way children are encouraged to define their day's play. One activity naturally leads into the next.

For example, from solitary sand play, the child may move along to the clay table or workbench where a cooperative project is underway. A leap off the swing may land her in the paddling pool. A race up the climber may lead to a quiet clubhouse meeting on top.

However, certain separations are vital, and this is where many of the commercial manufacturers err. It is unnatural and unsafe to try to cover all play needs with a single piece of equipment. It may seem practical, given space restrictions, to purchase an all-in-one climber (offering dangling gym equipment, multilevel decks, a hideaway on top and sandbox below), but you'll soon discover that it also offers some serious conflicts.

Picture three or more children using the climber at once: One child swings monkeylike through a tea party, scattering cups and unleashing the tea sipper's temper, who in turn unnerves the dreamer on the swing below, who in turn drops down to the sandbox and kicks another's five-story castle to bits.

"The children are only acting their age," says Polly Hill of the Canadian Children's Advisory Service. "The designer is the one who has built in these conflicts."

In general, the all-in-one structures present a very poor balance of activities, emphasizing the physical and ignoring the creative, cognitive and quiet sides of play. Both parents and children will pay in the end for blowing their entire budget on one massive jungle gym. Sure, it offers diverse opportunities to build muscles and test agility, but the experts who study public facilities have noted that children seldom stay occupied for more than a few minutes in such play. The other dimensions, by comparison, keep them engaged in a more concentrated manner for longer periods of time.

You can, however, vastly improve the play value of a jungle gym by adding constructive (loose) elements: a tarp lends privacy; found treasures and plain old junk can help in the improvising process.

Finding Loose Parts

Although making your own loose parts is a tradition among true adventurers, don't feel obliged to enroll in a woodworking course and set up shop in your basement. It's okay to buy loose parts. In fact, it can be more economical.

Many amateur builders end up spending a good deal more money making their own components than they might have spent buying them. If they love their hobby, it's probably worth the price to them. But don't be talked into it purely for economic reasons. I hear the same story over and over: "The sandbox was so easy to make, and so cheap." Funny how the story changes when the price includes a new router, power sander and the stack of timbers left over thanks to a major drafting error, plus the cost of the deluxe but totally unnecessary spring assembly that raises and lowers the lid, all of which add up to a $1,000 sandbox.

Shopping Around

For those who don't have the time or the manual ability to build their own, store-bought equipment is the safe and easy answer. And safety is a critical concern with home-built equipment. The do-it-yourselfer too often relies on his own design sense, ignoring safety considerations that guide most commercial manufacturers.

To get full value out of store-bought equipment, you must pay close attention to the materials used. The following are some of the things to look for when purchasing equipment for your children:

1. Unless you plan to keep play equipment indoors when not in use, select equipment designed specifically for outdoor play. If it is wood, it must be either chemically preserved or well sealed with at least three coats of outdoor paint or varnish.

While you will get the best wear out of unpainted, chemically treated wood, there is some debate about the toxicity of preservatives in general, even those advertised as nontoxic. Painted or lacquered wood is safer (make sure it contains no lead or chromium), but you may have to do periodic touch-ups.

The ultimate wood finish (favored by designers working with very big budgets) is synthetic resin in combination with nontoxic polyurethane paint. Kompan, a leading international play equipment manufacturer based in Denmark, uses this on its bonded fifteen-layer plywood panels for ultimate durability and good looks.

2. Choose equipment intended for residential use. There is no need to spend the extra money on gear designed to withstand heavy playground traffic. The standard commercial 1/4-inch galvanized chain used in playground swings is very costly and much stronger than you will require; rope is perfectly adequate for suspended equipment in your backyard. (More on rope selection, page 69.)

Similarly, the core logs and heavy 4 x 4 timbers commonly seen supporting public play structures are way out of scale with your yard, and really are not justified from a structural point of view. Carefully chosen fir 2 x 4s (with no knots) will support a large family of climbers for several years, providing the structure is secure and well balanced.

3. New-age plastics, such as polypropylene and polyethylene, are ideal for indoor–outdoor components because they are lightweight, weatherproof and durable. Their only drawback is that some molded plastic products are expensive: A rather ingenious toddler-sized circular ladder–slide in the Louise Kool + Galt catalog (Canada and England) costs over $300. The popular Little Tikes brand of molded polyethylene toys (sold in Canada, Britain and the United States) is also expensive, although many families — especially large ones — swear by them. The Little Tikes "big waffle" blocks and turtle sandboxes can withstand shocking abuse and come out showing no sign of wear and tear.

Best buys

In many cities you will find workshops, some of them operated by nonprofit organizations, that provide educational and play equipment to community centers, day-care centers and schools. It is hard to beat their prices. In fact, it's tough to build your own equipment for less. Here are some typical examples of basic wooden equipment from the Vancouver Community Workshop, a highly respected nonprofit operation in my neighborhood:

– **Toddler's ladder and slide assembly** connecting to a 2-square-foot platform, with crawl-through space below and handrails on top: $125 (design, page 88)

– **Convertible rock-and-row unit** with attached walking board, suitable for use by two- to ten-year-olds in a variety of different ways: $75

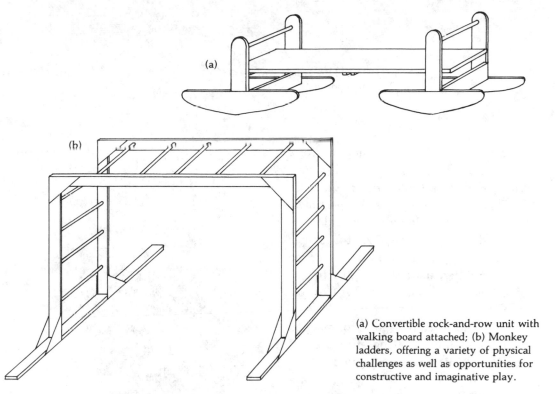

(a) Convertible rock-and-row unit with walking board attached; (b) Monkey ladders, offering a variety of physical challenges as well as opportunities for constructive and imaginative play.

– **Four-foot-tall puppet theater** that doubles as a lemonade stand, store front, post office or bank: $85

The best way to comparison shop for play equipment is through catalogs. It will give you a broad view of what is available, plus some great design ideas if you decide to build your own. Be sure, when requesting catalogs, to ask for current price lists – they are frequently, and not accidentally, omitted.

Here are a few of the standard commercial designs, suitable (with adaptations) for children of all ages:

Cleated Walking Boards: These are extremely easy to make (page 61), but they are also available commercially through school and day-care suppliers with nicely rounded corners and a tough, shiny finish. Alternatively, ask your neighborhood handyman to whip up a stack of them for you. They are best in sets of three or four, for building ramps, skyscrapers, slides and highways.

Monkey Ladder: This is a simple assembly of three wooden ladders – two vertical and one horizontal joining the two across the top, generally 5 to 6 feet tall. It is often used in schoolyards and gyms but is rarely seen in backyards, although it is one of the most versatile units for a physical workout as well as an ideal foundation for constructive play. With the addition of walking boards and a tarp, you have a multistory playhouse. Add a net for an extra climbing challenge. The options are endless.

Horizontal tire swing provides social opportunities.

Rope Ladder: When shopping for a rope ladder, look for sturdy nylon rope with plenty of extra length at both ends for fastening, and solid hardwood rungs. Or make it yourself with rope and hardwood dowels (see page 72 for simple design). A rope ladder can be suspended in many different ways—whether for access into a treehouse or fort, or for strength training.

Swings: Read Chapter 6 for more on building or buying swing structures. If you already have supports in your yard (a secure roof beam or suitable tree) it is easy to install loose swinging parts. Most playground suppliers sell belt-style swing seats; if you want to economize, avoid buying the chains—nylon rope is perfectly adequate for backyard swings.

Soft swing seats are better than rigid ones because they allow many more body positions and a greater degree of safe risk-taking. Tot swings with safety bars or chains are best for children younger than three (see design below).

Soft swing seats are versatile and safe.

A store-bought success: Kompan's Quadro seesaw, affording a multipositional ride for up to four children.

Alternate Swings: Your best swinging value for children age two and up is a tire swing, suspended horizontally by three ropes and attached at the top to a ball bearing swivel. (You can buy the whole assembly.) Taking up less room than conventional swings, the tire accommodates more children at once and a wider range of positions, offering increased physical and social dimensions.

The monkey swing — a plain wooden disk with rope strung through the center — is much cheaper than conventional swings and is loaded with play potential for all ages.

Spring Toys: These are the high tech answer to the old spring rocking horses. Because they are supported by a single heavy-gauge steel coil, you don't get the wild (often hazardous) ride of the lightweight ponies. This toy is meant to be anchored in the ground, usually by sinking a steel plate into a shallow hole, so the rider can't

flip or tip over. Also, the risk of finger pinching is eliminated with the giant coil. Installation is semipermanent; because no concrete is necessary, you can dig up the foundation and move the whole thing to another location.

A group of two or more spring toys is ideal for adding a social dimension to an otherwise solitary activity. It serves as a decent piece of complex equipment for children aged two to eight, providing a good physical workout, lots of room for imaginative play, and the social element. The drawback, however, is price—a spring toy can cost anywhere from $150 to $400.

Wombler: This giant plastic bowl goes by different names in different places, but a child's reaction to it is always the same—sheer delight. Up to four children can sit inside and, by rocking this way and that, "womble" clear across the lawn. They can even slide down a slope in it. It's great for winter sledding, or summer paddling. Turn it upside down for hide-and-seek, or pretend play.

...locomotion

Wheeled toys can make or break your backyard, so choose carefully. The key is to look for complex equipment, which automatically rules out trikes and bikes.

You will most likely end up buying your child some kind of bike in any case—who can resist? Just be clear about the distinction. A bike is merely a riding toy. It is invaluable on driveways and sidewalks, but makes a very small contribution to backyard play. In fact, bikes can easily detract from constructive and social play because they offer solitary activity that is out of proportion to the yard (they simply go too fast). Cooperation among young children with bikes is almost impossible when space is limited. Conflicts are inevitable.

By contrast, the following are examples of wheeled toys that serve important complex functions, inviting creativity and social interchange:

Tractor-dumper, wagon and wheelbarrow invite creativity and social interplay.

45

Wagon: It's a classic toy, for good reason. Durable plastic models are adequate for toddlers, but serious hauling calls for traditional steel-supported wagons on sturdy rubber wheels. Well built wooden wagons are as durable as metal ones, but are much heavier and usually more expensive.

Wheelbarrow: A proper toy wheelbarrow is as strong as the real garden variety, just smaller. Again, wood tends to be more cumbersome than metal. The classic American Radio Flyer metal model with wooden handles and a solid rubber wheel is unbeatable—it's strong enough for heavy loads and passengers. Besides being a handy earth mover, the wheelbarrow teaches children the principles of balance (the hard way).

A durable push cart: ideal as a doll buggy or earth mover

Dolly: Particularly handy on large decks and long sidewalks, the swivel-wheeled dolly is the most basic pull–push toy around. It should be at least 15 x 24 inches, to accommodate large stacks of blocks, buckets of water or a seated child. (There are a dozen different ways to ride a dolly, not all of them safe for toddlers. Rules may be necessary.)

Push Cart: This is not just a toddler's toy, although my own child actually learned to walk with hers. It can evolve over the years into a doll buggy, grocery cart or heavy earth mover, which is why you should look for durability at the outset. Galt "Toughies" are a wonderful line (sold in the United States, Canada and England), guaranteed to span generations. They are made with a tubular steel frame, timber sides and indestructible wheels.

Tractor/Dumper: You can choose from a variety. It is basically a riding toy propelled by feet or pedals, with an earth dumper on front or trailer on back, or both. Durable steel suspension is necessary if large loads will be carried or older children will be using the toy, as are swivel wheels or casters on the front for steering.

Toddler tractor: endless possibilities in a basic toy

From your local lumberyard

Older children should be included on shopping trips to lumber and hardware stores to take part in selecting the kind of loose parts they consider most valuable for their yard. The experience also allows them to visualize additions for future backyard projects, which is an ideal way to instill an appreciation for collecting things over time.

Your lumberyard shopping list might include any of the following:

Step Ladder: The standard A-frame (2 feet to 4 feet high) is invaluable as a structural support for all kinds of building projects, not to mention a base for homemade slides and access to climbing structures. (Rules for using a step ladder should be explicit for all age groups and discouraged for the very young child.)

Rung Ladder: As a versatile addition to climbing equipment, look for short ones (up to 5 feet) with hooks or cleats on one end. If toddlers are around, remove the lower one or two rungs to keep them on the ground where they belong.

Watering Equipment: If you don't already have the usual hose, sprinklers and watering cans, buy them now. Anyone who has observed children seriously playing with water will tell you there is no activity more physically and creatively engrossing. You can enhance water play by installing a tap assembly, with automatic shut-off, near the sandbox or clay table. (For more on water play, see page 129.)

Tarpaulins: Sling one over the monkey bars to make a clubhouse; toss another over the sandbox to keep the cats out. As long as they are sturdy and weatherproof (oilcloth or coated nylon) you will find dozens of uses for tarps.

Scrap Lumber: Look for bargain end pieces in plywood or chipboard—but no thicker than 5/8-inch or they get too heavy for kids to tote. Children under seven will use them primarily as walking boards and unnailed building components. They must be able to handle them without getting scraped by sharp corners or jabbed by splinters, so finish all the pieces by rounding cut edges. Sand and seal well with non-toxic waterproof paint or varnish. Add cleats (page 61) for secure use as ramps or balance boards. Under supervision, older children can simply bang away at unfinished soft woods—pine is ideal.

Landscape Ties: These are the 4 x 6 cores of plywood logs, generally hemlock or fir, cut to standard 8-1/2-foot lengths. If you can't find them in a lumberyard, call a landscape architect or contractor and ask for their best source.

Although many landscapers use them by the ton, ties are actually a surplus by-product of building lumber and are therefore relatively cheap (five to seven dollars a tie). Because they come pretreated to resist ground rot, ties are ideal for use as retaining structures, foundation posts and balance beams. (Avoid creosote-treated ties, and use caution even with the "nontoxic" treated ties—they are best suited to ground structures that are not being constantly handled by children.)

Scavenging With Skill

When it comes to playthings, the art of scavenging truly pays off—not only by saving you money, but by adding immeasurable intrigue to your collection of loose parts. There is nothing more valuable to a child than a found treasure. Call it junk if you will—just don't let your kids catch you throwing it away.

Scavenging is easy, once you become familiar with the sources. Don't expect to just wander down the street and find useful stuff—that might happen once, but rarely twice and never three times. Artful scavengers know they have to wander far and wide for true treasures (they often start by letting their fingers do the walking, through the Yellow Pages). They also, at times, have to pay for the good stuff. In fact, some items may seem awfully expensive—for *junk*—but when you compare them to their store-bought equivalents, they'll seem like bargains.

Children are natural scavengers. Encourage them to keep their eyes open for valuable contributions to the yard. To spare hurt feelings and major embarrassments, be sure to teach them the difference between scavenging, garbage collection and theft.

Listed are some of the hottest scavenging sources:

— Garage Sales: For the serious scavenger, shopping garage sales is a way of life. Read the classifieds. Stalk the neighborhoods with the most kids. Get to the sales early.

— Schools: You'd be surprised what some schools and day-care centers have in their storage rooms. Old gym equipment, chipped tables, lopsided easels—which, in many cases, they'll let go for the right price or just for the convenience of having somebody cart it away. I've seen an entire playground furnished for free with discarded tubular steel climbing equipment that some gym teacher thought was "out of fashion." Installed properly with safe ground cover, that was a real found treasure.

— Shipping Companies: Packing crates make perfect platforms, or disassemble easily for soft (though rough) scrap wood.

— Dairies: Plastic milk bottle cases are virtually indestructible—they make great basic building blocks for your yard, or handy storage units. If you are lucky, the dairy will part with old ones for free. Call around.

— Excavators–Tree fellers–Landscape Contractors: Blasted rock is particularly nice as a border treatment because you get lots of irregular shapes and coloration. Smooth river rocks are better if small children are about. Stumps can be used in a hundred ways—as lawn furnishings, climbing structures, steps and retaining walls. In wet climates, score the cut surface and seal with epoxy resin to prevent slippery moss from presenting a climbing hazard. Generally you can have these things for free, but you've got to figure out a way of carting them home.

— Wire and Cable Companies: You might find a company willing to part with a wooden cable spool or two. You've really hit the jackpot if you get one for free. Generally, companies use spools until they fall apart (new ones can cost hundreds of dollars) and then sell the dilapidated hulks back to the suppliers who remake them. Your best bet is to have a friend at the yard who is able to help you when one becomes available. If you can get one of these hardwood spools, you can do all kinds of nifty things with it at home.

Large spools can be converted to play-houses by removing several slats and cutting holes for windows.

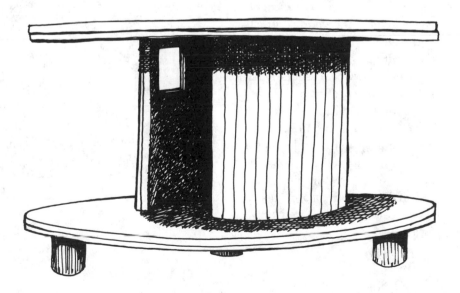

The best spool for use as a table, climbing component or building block is the 36-inch (diameter) size, which stands about 2 feet on end. The larger spools make great little playhouses: just remove a few of the center staves to create a doorway. You can mount them on blocks for a raised fort, or place one on top of another for a cable tower. But be sure to ask for cable spools. Wire spools are not finished as smoothly and often have open spaces around their core.

— Barrel Manufacturers–Oil Companies–Distilleries: Barrels and drums are among the most versatile and developmentally valuable playthings around. Large ones (like the 50-gallon oil drum) make great rolling toys and tunnels when the ends are removed. You should have the ends industrially cut away and the jagged edge carefully rolled back—a difficult job at home. Metal drums will also need to be thoroughly cleaned with solvent before (ideally) being sanded and painted with a tough all-weather finish to reduce rusting.

Wooden barrels are easier to work with, but not nearly as sturdy in the long run. Look for barrels with hoops so you can tighten the slats as the wood contracts with age. It also helps to seal them with an epoxy resin to keep moisture out. Check regularly for splinters or protrusions. Both wood and metal barrels can be sunk in a few inches of sand for more comfortable tunnel play for toddlers, supported off the ground with tires or blocks for older children, or propped in a slide position for children of all ages.

Barrels or drums, safely finished, are one of the most versatile playthings around.

— Appliance Dealers: Though not durable, giant cardboard stove or refrigerator boxes can occupy children for days. Let them design their own playhouses, cars or space stations by first drafting them on paper, and then marking the required cuts with pencils or felts on the cardboard boxes. You'll have to help with the cutting (exacto blades work best). Add a fancy paint job, paper shingles, a steering wheel, cloth curtains—whatever accessories can be found.

— Gas Stations, Auto Dealers–Wreckers, Retreaders: Finding a source for scrap tires is no problem. Neither is finding a use for them in your play yard. The only limitation is aesthetic—too many old tires lying around the yard is bound to give the appearance of a dump (not that the kids would mind).

Avoid steel belting. It is very hard to cut through and can poke out of the rubber over time, creating a hazard. Bus and truck tires are best for swings or climbing components. Tires from tractors or earth-moving equipment can be used as sandboxes, the top opening enlarged by cutting off 6 inches all the way around. In all cases, scrub the tires first with brush and abrasive cleanser. Drill drain holes. (Turn to page 65 for a number of basic tire designs.)

CHAPTER 5

Building The Basics

Children older than six can be of tremendous help in building or assembling play equipment. And there is no better place to start than with loose parts, which are generally smaller and simpler in design than the climbers and playhouses in the following chapter. In fact, even tiny children can pitch in here — with safe jobs like sanding, painting and snack patrol. All you need is patience, and a strict code of rules.

Tools and Tips

If you are not fully competent with tools yourself, don't attempt to train or supervise children. Find an old hand in the neighborhood who wouldn't mind spending an hour or two with the lot of you. All you need is a little dexterity to get off to a safe start.

Your eventual goal may be to let the children take over the job completely. To do this, remove yourself very gradually, until you can supervise from a safe (shouting) distance. Never leave children entirely unattended.

The right size and weight of tools are crucial for children to ensure both safety and good results. Frustration is inevitable among novice builders, but if tools are way out of scale with little hands, frustration will only increase and the children will not learn properly. Even with small, simple tools it is essential to practise, delaying big projects until everyone can saw straight and drive their nails true.

You will need the following:
- stable workbench (to build your own, see page 55)
- storage for tools and wood
- 3 or 4 wooden orange crates or similar containers for small work stations and storage

— framing hammer, 7 to 10 oz., 12 inches long, with wooden handle
— cross-cut saw for the main cuts, with 12-inch tempered steel blade
— keyhole saw for finer jobs, with a narrow 10-inch blade
— level
— brace and drill, preferably 16- x 16-inch, high-carbon auger bit and alligator jaws
— screwdriver
— box chisel
— wood rasp
— combination square
— clamps
— measuring tape
— wood glue and filler
— putty knife
— assorted sandpaper
— paintbrushes
— paint and lacquers of choice
— assorted box of nails, tacks and screws
— carpenter's apron (easy to improvise by hemming up an old kitchen apron to form a shallow pocket for nails and loose bits)
— pencils and paper
— first-aid kit

(Most of these supplies can be purchased at a hardware store or lumberyard.)

Some basic construction tips

—Wood: Select wood carefully, choosing outdoor grades where appropriate. Foundation timbers must be chemically treated, but in wet climates you should use treated (nontoxic) woods for the entire project. Solid fir is best for support. Plywood is better than particle board for panels because it is lighter and holds screws better. Pine is soft and lightweight.

—Surfaces: Fill any cracks, knots or irregularities in the wood. Miter the edges and corners wherever possible; sand smooth and seal with at least two coats of outdoor paint or polyurethane lacquer, sanding between coats. In wet climates, consider spending a little extra on marine enamel or spar varnish—these tough finishes are better looking and are a better value in the long run.

Sanding blocks may be useful in large projects: Simply fold a piece of sandpaper around three sides of a 6 x 2 wood block and tack firmly.

—Wood Measurements: Keep in mind that the listed stock sizes are not the same as the actual measurements of the wood you buy in a lumberyard. A 2 x 4 actually measures 1-1/2 inches by 3-1/2 inches. Draft your plans accordingly.

—Safety: The most crucial factor in childproof construction is the prevention of head entrapment. When gaps between 4 inches and 9 inches are left in climbing equipment, on platforms or between the rungs of ladders, children's bodies can fall through but their heads may get lodged, resulting in strangulation or broken necks. So be sure to keep openings less than 4 inches wide, or more than 9 inches.

—Joints: Take time to glue and nail or screw all joints. The strongest for wood bonding is a resorcinol or formaldehyde adhesive (the former is best in wet areas, and neither should be used by children). Clamp glued joints for at least three hours to set, then fasten with hardware appropriate to thickness and structural placement of the wood. Countersink heads, and fill the holes with plastic wood.

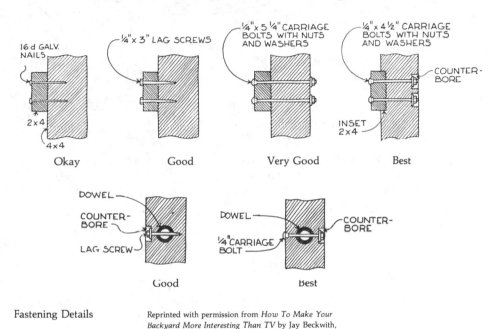

Fastening Details

Reprinted with permission from *How To Make Your Backyard More Interesting Than TV* by Jay Beckwith, McGraw-Hill Book Co., 1980

Ready to build

An appropriate first project is the workbench, because building it will not only give the physical setup you'll need for further handiwork, but will also give a good deal of practice in the fine arts of sawing and banging.

1. Workbench and Nail Box

Not everyone will have a convenient location for a junior carpentry shop outdoors. If you don't, the garage or basement will certainly suffice, though there is something positively invigorating about working with wood outdoors. The relatively compact size of this bench may allow both options: put it on the back porch or deck during project hours, then tuck it out of sight when it is not needed.

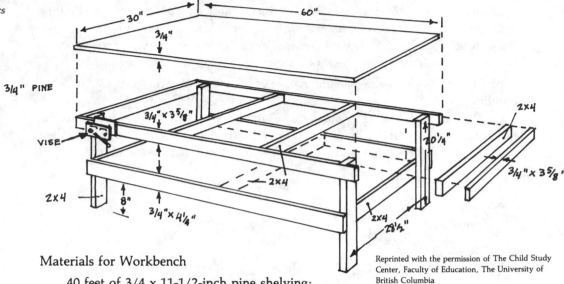

Reprinted with the permission of The Child Study Center, Faculty of Education, The University of British Columbia

Materials for Workbench

40 feet of 3/4 x 11-1/2-inch pine shelving:
- cut 2 end pieces 3-5/8 x 27 inches
- 2 upper horizontals 3-5/8 x 60 inches
- 2 middle horizontals 4-1/4 x 55-1/4 inches
- shelf, 2 pieces 11-1/2 x 52 inches and 1 piece 5-1/2 x 52 inches
- top, 2 pieces 11-1/2 x 60 inches and 1 piece 7 x 60 inches

24 feet of 2 x 4s:
- 4 legs 20-1/4 inches long
- 4 end and 3 center horizontals, 28-1/2 inches long
- wood vise

For nail box

5 feet of 1/2 x 3-inch pine:
- 2 ends and 2 dividers, 2-3/8 x 5 inches
- 2 sides, 2-3/8 x 18-1/8 inches

1/8-inch masonite for box bottom:
- cut 6 x 18-1/8 inches

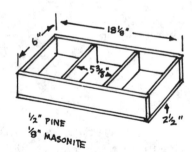

Construction

To construct the workbench, start by framing the two 28-1/2-inch ends, screwing the lower horizontals inside the legs and the double upper horizontals outside the legs — ends flush. Join ends with 3-5/8 x 60-inch horizontals; add 4-1/4 x 55-1/4-inch horizontals below. Screw one 2 x 4 to support the shelf and two 2 x 4s to support the top. Drill the bench to attach wood vise. Nail on shelf boards, then top. Sand and finish.

For the nail box, nail ends to sides; add bottom and dividers. Sand and finish.

2. Sawhorse

The sawhorse is not only a builders' aid, but a very handy loose part that can support planks in a climbing structure, boards for balancing or sliding, and countless other play components. Here is the simplest sawhorse design I have found:

Materials for sawhorse

12 feet of 2 x 4 hardwood:
— 4 legs, 24 inches each
— top, 46 inches
22 x 5-inch piece of 3/4-inch plywood
2-1/2-inch nails

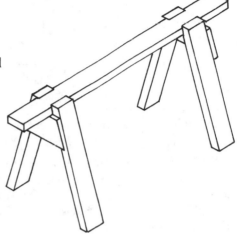

Reprinted with permission from *Improvised Playthings* by Margaret Ellis and Brian Nielsen, The University of Alberta Press, 1980

Construction

Saw, chisel or rasp grooves in the top bar for the legs, beginning 6-1/2 inches from each end, running 3-1/2 inches long and 1/2 inch deep at the top. Hold a leg in place in the groove and measure the triangle to be cut off the top of the leg to make it

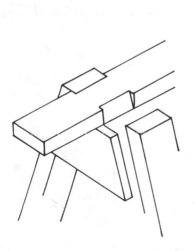

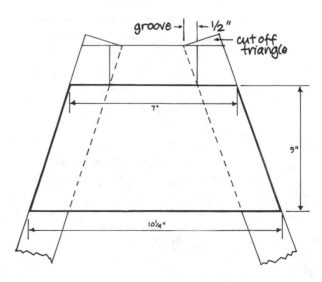

57

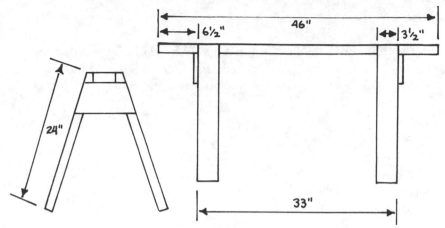

flush with the top bar. Trim the legs, top and bottom. Attach one pair of legs at a time, first with glue, then nails (use screws if the sawhorse is going to be supporting much weight or be used as a play component later). While glue sets, measure each plywood leg brace and cut. Repeat for second set of legs. Fill flaws, sand and finish.

It is easy to vary the height of the sawhorse by changing the angle of the grooves in the top bar. Add rubber strips on the feet for use on indoor floors.

(It is even easier to buy sawhorse braces at a lumberyard, and just cut 2 x 4s to the dimensions you require.)

3. Cleated Ladder

A 5-foot ladder is tall enough to give most children a climbing challenge, but still manageable enough to be freely moved about the play area for a wide variety of purposes. The top piece provides a cleat for securing the ladder against platforms. When used as a bridge, you must provide additional center support.

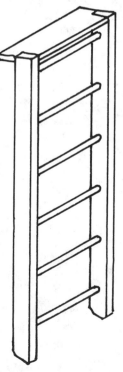

Materials for cleated ladder

    10 feet of 2 x 4:
    — 2 legs, 5 feet each
    9 feet of 1-inch dowel:
    — 6 rungs, 18 inches each
    — 1 piece of 1-inch plywood, 7 x 18-3/4 inches, for cleat
    — wood screws, 1-1/2 inches and 2 inches
    — wood glue
    — wood filler
    — paint and lacquer

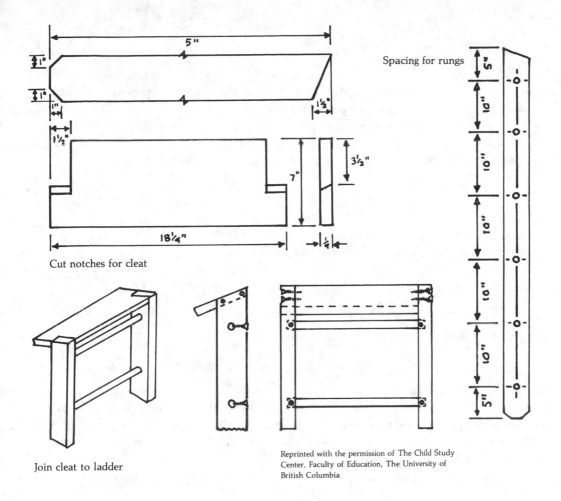

Spacing for rungs

Cut notches for cleat

Join cleat to ladder

Reprinted with the permission of The Child Study Center, Faculty of Education, The University of British Columbia

Construction

Cut the 2 x 4 in half, then trim ends. Cut out two of the plywood corners to allow the ladder legs to fit into the cleat. Drill 1-inch diameter holes exactly 1 inch deep into the legs (you can scale the ladder to the size of your children, but remember to keep rungs a minimum of 9 inches apart to prevent head entrapment). Glue rungs into sides, and top piece onto top of legs. Clamp until dry, making sure the legs are parallel and even.

Drill small lead holes through the edge of the legs into the rungs. Insert 1-1/2-inch wood screws to prevent rungs from twisting or rolling. Insert 2-inch screws through the sides of the legs into the edge of the plywood top piece. Fill, sand and finish.

Finish the ladder's feet with weather mat or rubber stripping to prevent slipping or damage to indoor floors. Cleats may also be made of bent strap iron.

4. Notched Blocks

These versatile connecting blocks make log cabins, peaked fortresses, farmyards and railway systems. If you have a large patio or deck, one set of notched blocks will fill it with an entire miniature city.

It is tempting to paint the blocks in a variety of bright colors, but developmentalists argue for a single muted shade. Varied colors can dictate a child's choices with toys like these, imposing certain order and form. A noncolor gives the child complete creative freedom.

Materials

Suggested quantities for a full set:
(all pieces cut from 3/4-inch outdoor-grade plywood)

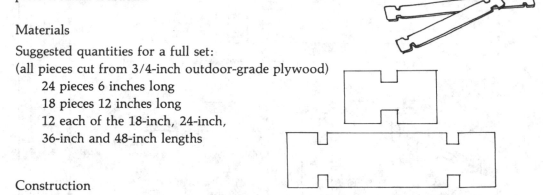

24 pieces 6 inches long
18 pieces 12 inches long
12 each of the 18-inch, 24-inch,
36-inch and 48-inch lengths

Construction

The pattern is simple, but it calls for a great deal of cutting. Professional tools would definitely come in handy, especially if you want a large set of blocks. Or go halfway by paying a lumberyard clerk to do the rough cutting while you finish the job at home with keyhole saw, chisel or rasp, and sander and paints. Little helper hands can come in very handy.

Cut plywood to the dimensions shown, notching each piece top and bottom,

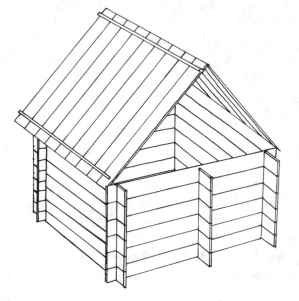

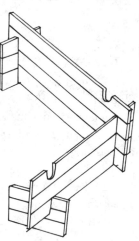

Reprinted with the permission of The Child Study Center, Faculty of Education, The University of British Columbia.

5/8 inch wide and 1 inch deep. The shortest (6-inch) panels should only be notched in the center. The others need 4 notches, 2-1/2 inches from each end. For variety, notch some of these longer blocks in the center as well. All blocks are 4 inches wide, varying only in length and number of notches. Quantity can be determined by the amount of plywood you can afford (scrap pieces are fine). Sand well and finish.

5. Walking Boards or Teeters

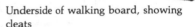

You take a board, add cleats and presto! The most basic loose part you can make. Once you get the hang of it, make lots more.

Underside of walking board, showing cleats

Materials

1-inch plywood, cut to desired width (minimum 7 inches):
  — cut to 7 feet 8 inches long for teeter board
  — any suitable length for walking–balancing boards
1 x 1-inch fir or alder stripping for cleats:
  — cut to width of board

Construction

To attach to a climbing structure, measure the cleats to fit the appropriate bars or timbers. For use as a teeter board, place cleats in the center to fit gate rod (see 6.) or the top bar of a sawhorse.

Secure cleats with countersunk screws, round edges of the boards, fill and sand well to prevent slivers. Seal and finish.

6. Play Gate

This piece of equipment is so basic, you should make at least two of them. One play gate can be used to support a teeter board or slide, two to anchor a walking board or platform, others as ladders or (as you'd expect) gates.

Materials

5 feet of 2 x 4 fir:
  — cut two 30-inch legs
  4 feet of 3 x 3-inch fir:
  — cut two 24-inch support planks
  7-1/2 feet of 1-inch hardwood dowelling:
  — cut three 30-inch bars
  — 1-1/2-inch wood screws, 1/4 x 4-1/2-inch carriage bolts with nuts and washers, tie-rods

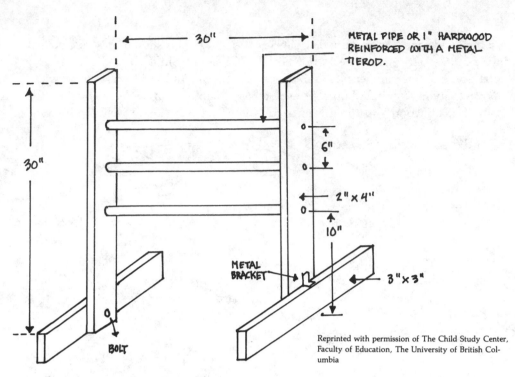

METAL PIPE OR 1" HARDWOOD REINFORCED WITH A METAL TIEROD.

30"

30"

6"

2" x 4"

10"

METAL BRACKET

3" x 3"

BOLT

Reprinted with permission of The Child Study Center, Faculty of Education, The University of British Columbia

Construction

Whatever their use, play gates must be durable and well balanced. Cut and finish fir frame, attach dowels (metal pipe may be used for extra strength), using same method as for ladder (above) but reinforced here with metal tie-rods. Bolt legs to support planks. For extra reinforcement, attach a standard metal bracket (available at any hardware store) to the outside of each lower leg joint, as shown.

7. Swivel Board

Making the swivel board is basically an exercise in drilling wood. The result is a movable balance beam that can also be an elevated highway cutting through a sand city, or the basis of a geometry quiz. It is infinitely more complex than the usual single-beam balance units.

Materials

4 feet of 2-1/2 x 5-1/4-inch solid fir or pine:
— cut four 1-foot blocks
11 feet of 7/8 x 4-inch fir or stair-tread lumber:
— cut three 44-inch planks
3 feet of 1-inch dowelling:
— cut twelve 3-inch pieces

Construction

You can order the wood precut from the lumberyard, but if you'd like to see some skin left on those little ankles be sure to round the corners and edges of the planks. The holes in the blocks are cut 1-1/4 inches deep and 1-1/16 inches wide to snugly take the dowelling plus glue. The holes in the planks must be 1/4 inch wider to allow swivelling. Precise placement of holes is not crucial.

Reprinted with the permission of The Child Study Center, Faculty of Education, The University of British Columbia

8. Rocking Boat

This is actually much more than a boat. This classic complex toy provides a vehicle for countless imaginary voyages, a soothing place to rock oneself quietly into oblivion, a great seating area for sing-songs plus (when overturned) a climbing–jumping structure for more physical pursuits. The dimensions below make a small two-seater. For a larger boat, make the steps 35-1/2 inches long rather than 23-3/4 inches; the top step should be 17-1/2 inches, and small steps 10-1/4 inches wide. Use 3/4-inch plywood for sides and steps in larger model.

Materials

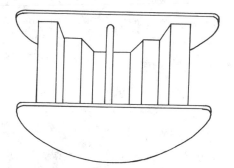

    3/4-inch plywood:
    — cut 2 side pieces, 48 x 14 inches
    1-inch hardwood dowelling, 19-1/2 inches long
    1/2-inch plywood:
    — cut 4 steps, 8 x 23-3/4 inches
    — cut base 12 x 23-3/4 inches
    15 feet of quarter-round wood stripping

Construction

Draw the boat shape onto plywood sides, then saw and sand smooth. Chisel out grooves for the ends of the four stepboards and the base board, 3/8-inch deep, into the inside of the plywood sides. Inset steps and base into sides and glue into

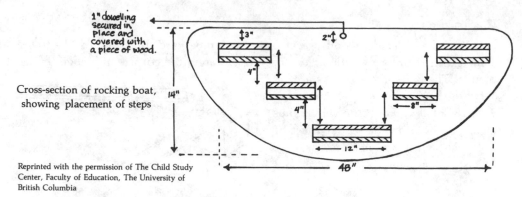

Cross-section of rocking boat, showing placement of steps

1" dowelling secured in place and covered with a piece of wood.

Reprinted with the permission of The Child Study Center, Faculty of Education, The University of British Columbia

place. Strengthen the steps by nailing 16 supports of quarter-round, 8 inches long, to the plywood sides, above and below the ends of each step board. Strengthen the base similarly, using 4 supports of quarter-round, each 12 inches long.

Inset, glue and screw the dowelling across the center of boat as a handbar. You may want to secure it further by cutting two 2-inch-wide circles of wood and nailing them over the ends of the crossbar on the outside of the plywood. Sand and finish.

9. Dolly or Scooter Board

The most basic and versatile wheeled toy is a piece of plywood on casters. With a grain of ingenuity, that's all the instruction you will need to make one (why not a few?) of them. To make a deluxe model that swivels, stacks and doesn't scratch your walls:

Materials (for a single 1-foot-square board)
    3/4-inch plywood, cut to 12 x 12 inches
    4 swivel casters
    16 wood screws, 1/2- to 3/4-inch size
    woodfiller and paint
    48 inches of 3/4-inch wide plastic tape for edges, or bike tire
    floor flange and 18-inch section of 1-inch dowel for stacking model

Scooter boards are easily cut in different shapes. The center hole allows stacking.

Reprinted with permission from *Improvised Playthings* by Margaret Ellis and Brian Nielsen, The University of Alberta Press, 1980

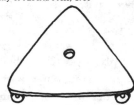

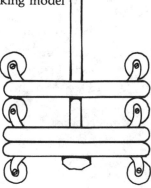

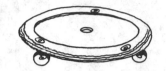

Old bicycle tire

Construction

Start by rounding the corners and edges of the board, filling flaws, sanding and finishing. (Scooters don't have to be square. Experiment with a round or triangular board.) Use the casters to mark screw locations, then drill small lead holes. Screw casters in place. Tape edges or make a bumper by attaching an old bike tire with screws and washers. You can also soften the ride by gluing a scrap of carpet or underlay onto the wood surface.

For a set of stacking scooters, drill a 1-inch hole in the centers of them all, screw a floor flange to the underside of one and insert a removable post (1-inch dowel will do). The other boards will stack up neatly on this one. Casters must be regularly oiled.

Building With Tires

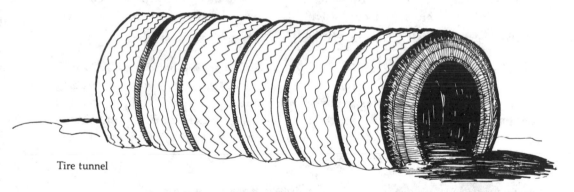

Tire tunnel

See page 51 for instructions on choosing tires and preparing them for play. No further handiwork is necessary for simple tire structures. One of the most popular playthings at an elementary school near my house is a tunnel of tractor tires partially sunk into soft earth. (If you want to make such a tunnel for toddlers, keep it short enough to allow an adult to quickly reach a stuck or frightened child.) By changing the configuration, you can build a crawl-through playhouse or maze.

Always remember to make drain holes in tires, using a hollow punch and hammer or 1-inch auger bit.

Joining and suspending tires has become something of a folk art in recent years. Show me a well-built public playground that doesn't have at least one tire ladder, bouncer or swing. You can pay good money to buy tire equipment fully assembled

TOP VIEW

Crawl-through playhouse

from playground suppliers; or, you can make your own, very simply, virtually for pennies.

Whether you are joining tread to tread, sidewall to sidewall or tread to sidewall, you should bolt the tires together with the following hardware:

one 3/8 x 2-inch hex cap screw
two 3/8-inch nuts
two 3/8-inch heavy-duty fender washers
two 3/4-inch steel washers
one 3/8-inch lock washer

You can make a 3/8-inch hole by either punching through the tire (use a 2 x 4 to support it from the inside) with a hammer and a 7/16-inch hollow punch. Or use a power drill and 7/16-inch auger bit with the square end cut off—if you don't have chain cutters, get a hardware store to cut the end for you, so it will fit into the power drill.

To suspend tires: Rope is generally strong enough for backyards—3/4-inch manila or 1/2-inch nylon can safely support up to 1,000 pounds. If you are attaching a multi-tire structure to a tree or support beams and expect several children to climb on it at once, cable is the stronger choice (1/4-inch cable is five times stronger than manila rope). For cable, use simple hardware clamps rather than knots, and tape cut ends with plastic or electrical tape.

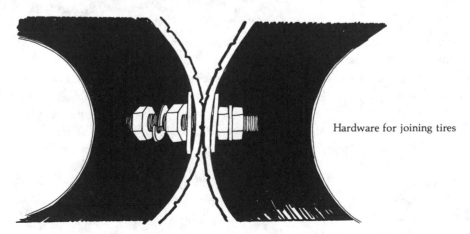

Hardware for joining tires

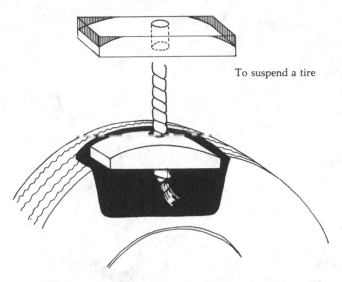

To suspend a tire

The most popular suspended tire is the swing. Choose a nonradial truck or bus tire for adequate rigidity. To hang it vertically: Cut a 12-inch length of 2 x 4 to the contour of the inside of the tread. Drill a hole through the center of the wood and the tread. Pass rope through both and knot it, using a round turn and two half-hitches (see page 70). Or pass cable through the tire, the wood and a 3/4-inch steel washer, then clamp.

Horizontal tire swings on a swivel

To suspend the tire horizontally: Cut three 4-inch lengths of 3 x 3-inch hardwood and round the corners slightly so that they fit snugly into the sidewall of a truck or bus tire. Drill three holes through sidewall and wood, about 2 inches from the tread. Cut cable or rope long enough to run from one hole through the swivel and out to a second hole. Tie or clamp under the wood and at the top near the swivel to prevent slipping. Cut a second length to run from the last hole up to the swivel, and clamp or tie at the top. The swivel (available at low cost from most hardware) should be at least 3 feet above the tire. Rope ends should again be knotted with a round turn and two half-hitches, while taped cable ends should be secured inside the tire with 3/4-inch steel washer and clamp.

Multi-tire swings, ladders and climbers

are easily constructed using a combination of these techniques. But your first concern is a secure place to suspend them. When using trees, seek expert advice about the strength of limbs. Also take care not to to let rope or cable injure the tree by wearing it down at contact points. A rubber sleeve—even a scrap piece of tire—can be used as a shield between rope or cable and limb.

You can attach tire structures to vertical supports by using large fence staples for cable, or lag bolts under rope. Freestanding support posts must be sunk at least 30 percent of their height into the ground, to a minimum depth of 2 feet. More on safe installation on page 87.

Once you get the knack of joining tires, any number of configurations can be made.

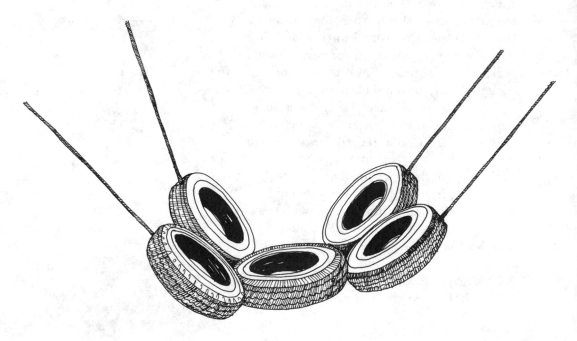

Safety tips for swings:
- Tire swings should be suspended no more than 3 feet above ground;
- Swings and climbers should be installed over safe impact surface;
- Swings must have a clear area in every direction to avoid collisions with passers-by or other swingers;
- Multi-tire climbers must be supported from the top as well as the sides to prevent tipping;
- Wrap cut cable ends with plastic or electrical tape.

Commonsense safety rules must be followed when playing with rope or suspended equipment:
- Whip games are often hazardous and should be watched carefully or outlawed entirely;
- Daredevil feats such as tightrope walking and tarzan leaping should be closely supervised;
- Loose rope should not be left lying (or hanging) about where very young children can become entangled.

On the other hand, don't let anxiety over potential accidents get in the way of adventure-play with rope. Just do it sensibly.

All About Rope

Familiarize yourself with rope and you'll add an enormous dimension to the play yard. It's a loose part that literally ties all the other parts together. Types of rope are listed below:

- Nylon is the strongest, most resilient rope for lashing and supporting heavy weight, but it is hardest on your hands. It will cause skin burn if used for hand-over-hand climbing, sliding or tarzan-style swinging. It also stretches with wear (as much as 40 percent), which can present problems with lashings.
- Terylene is almost as strong as nylon, but its greater weight makes it less practical for small jobs.
- Polypropylene and polyethylene are favored in backyards. Although they are the weakest of the man-made ropes, 1/2- to 5/8-inch thicknesses are certainly strong enough for most backyard purposes. They are gentler on skin, stretch less than nylon and are very lightweight.
- Natural fibers are kindest of all to the skin, stretch little, and are generally cheaper than the synthetics. They are much weaker, however, and in key support areas must be regularly inspected and replaced, at least once a year. Common choices are manila and sisal, in 3/4-inch width.

All rope will fray if cut ends are left. Synthetic fibers should be melted together; natural rope should be spliced, clamped or tightly wrapped with fine wire and tape.

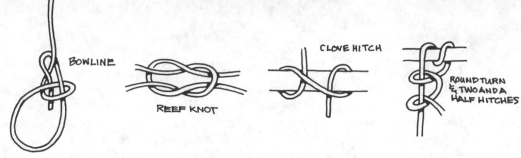

...common knots

— The bowline is a very safe loop knot, which should never collapse. Use it for tying rope to a tree (cushioned with rubber) or for making loops to swing on.

— The clove hitch is used when the rope attaches to an object and then continues on in the same direction. It is commonly used for net climbing structures.

— A reef knot is the safest for joining two different strands.

— A round turn and two half hitches are used to secure a rope to a frame, or for attaching a swing or other object to the rope.

...some simple rope projects

1. Rope Swings

The most basic but most challenging swing in the world is a length of rope suspended loosely between vertical supports. Depending on the slack, kids can sit, stand and (with practice) even walk on the rope. Attach to trees or supports with lag bolts plus rubber cushioning to prevent wear.

A tarzan swing is simply a knotted length of hanging rope. In a large yard with good impact surfacing, kids will figure out a dozen positions and applications.

Small children are better off using a monkey swing—the same principle but with a round wooden plate rather than knots to sit or stand on. For a softer alternative, tie a durable canvas sack filled with sawdust to the end of the rope.

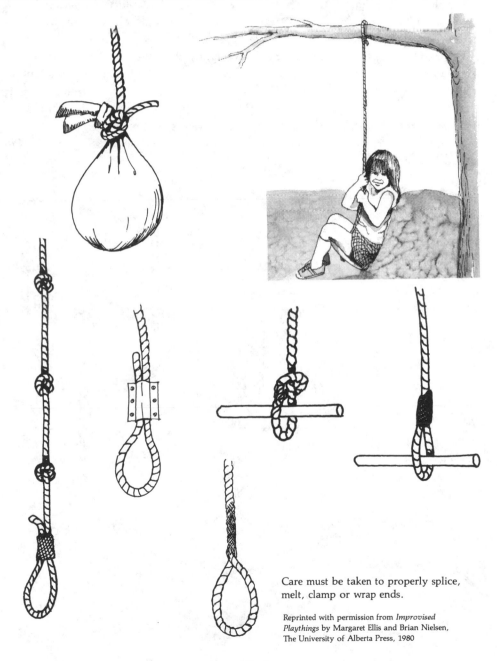

Care must be taken to properly splice, melt, clamp or wrap ends.

Reprinted with permission from *Improvised Playthings* by Margaret Ellis and Brian Nielsen, The University of Alberta Press, 1980

71

2. Gym Equipment

Replace or supplement a regular swing with a trapeze and rings set for extra challenge. For the trapeze, cut a 16-inch length of 1-inch hardwood dowel for the bar; drill 1/2-inch holes an inch from each end. Sand and finish. Use a single piece of 1/2-inch rope, determining length according to stature and ability of children. Leave an extra 2 feet of rope for the knots and assembly. Feed each rope end through a hole in the dowel and knot it separately. To attach trapeze to overhead bar, loop the top end of the rope over the bar and pass the dowel down through the loop.

Rings are made by threading 1/2-inch rope through an 8-inch length of rubber hose or tubing. Bring end up to form a loop, splicing or clamping securely. The joint must be strong and smooth, to avoid injury. The joint as well as tubing should be wrapped tightly with cloth tape to provide a good grip and protect against splitting. Splice or clamp the tops of each rope separately, and suspend using appropriate method.

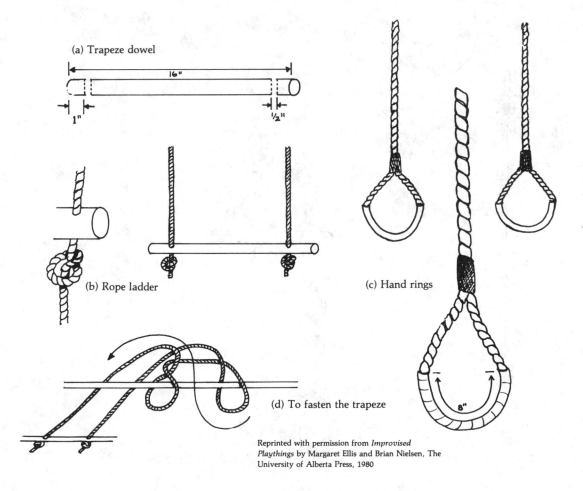

(a) Trapeze dowel

16"

1"   1/2"

(b) Rope ladder

(c) Hand rings

(d) To fasten the trapeze

8"

Reprinted with permission from *Improvised Playthings* by Margaret Ellis and Brian Nielsen, The University of Alberta Press, 1980

3. Rope Ladder

This is just like making the trapeze, over and over again. Start with a suitable number of 16-inch lengths of 1-inch hardwood dowel (depending on desired height of ladder). Measure the 1/2-inch rope by doubling the desired height, and adding an extra 9 to 11 feet for knots and assembly.

Drill 1/2-inch holes in either side of the dowels, 1 inch from each end. Feed both rope ends through the holes in the first rung, sliding the rung up to form a loop that measures 7 feet around. Tie bowline knots under the dowel on each side and continue adding rungs until you reach desired height. Hang the ladder in the same manner as trapeze. To make it more secure for very young children, stake the ends into the ground.

CHAPTER 6

King of the Castle

L arge structures have their place — especially in large yards. Developmentalists may argue that you get more value per square inch with small movable pieces, but if you've got enough space you can have it both ways. After all, developmentalists aren't the ones who use the monkey bars, playhouses, gym sets and tree forts. Children do, and when these structures are well designed they can offer tremendous challenge and enjoyment.

There is a certain value — more accurately, a thrill — in climbing as high and getting as far out of sight as you possibly can. It is hard to be king of the castle on a sawhorse.

Buying the Right Climber

The most popular modern play structure is often referred to as a climber, although these all-in-one units actually offer a lot more activities than climbing. You can get swings, slides, ladders and decks all supported on the single frame. When creatively designed, climbers offer a wide range of complex play options, making the steep price worthwhile. As an added bonus, you can usually customize climbers to your own yard, increasing their life span by adding more challenging features (like gym components) as your children grow.

A serious drawback to the 'more the merrier' philosophy of many manufacturers is the awkward and frequently hazardous crowding of incompatible features. You might find the slide landing area intersecting with the swinging arc, or a horizontal ladder over a sand-play area.

So choose carefully. Comparison shop using catalogs from regional and national manufacturers. Read the fine print about such things as material specifications, installation, surfacing and safety features. You'd be surprised how much you

A well-built, playground-style climber
for backyards with room to spare

can learn about design and function by studying the options. If a particular model interests you, call the manufacturer or retail outlet to find out if one has been installed near your home so you can observe it in use. (If you are an ambitious do-it-yourselfer, catalogs are an invaluable source of design ideas.)

The old-style metal swing sets may seem like a real bargain compared to the newer designed climbers (which can easily cost two or three times as much). In fact, swing sets are often severely limited in play value, which means less for your money. Generally, swing sets come equipped with rigid toddler-sized swings and tiny slides that bore most four-year-olds.

A well built climber, on the other hand, has much greater stability and can support a proper slide and belt or tire swings that move in a wider arc. Many models come with a variety of add-ons, to replace or supplement swinging. And, unlike swing sets, climbers are meant to be climbed on, through and over — which children will inevitably try to do on flimsy swing sets as well, despite serious risks.

Unless you have, or plan to have, several young children, think twice before purchasing a toddler-sized climber. They're great in public parks where the neighborhoods generate an endless supply of toddlers, but not in your average backyard. Your own toddlers are guaranteed to outgrow their low-slung climber before you've even made the last bank payment. Children master play equipment surprisingly quickly when they get to work out on it daily.

To make sure your investment pays off, look for a climber built for serious (but safe) challenges—structures tall enough to support climbing ropes and firemen poles, strong enough to top with a crow's nest playhouse or observatory, and versatile enough to accommodate cleated boards and tarps for construction projects.

To make a large climber safe for toddlers, you can easily install lower handrails, add ramps for easy access to safe, low decks and remove lower ladder rungs to keep them from climbing up. (See Appendix III, page 176 for young children's body dimensions.)

No matter what the ages of the children using the climber, certain rules must apply. You must decide which decks can and can't be leapt from. Swinging might be curtailed in the presence of toddlers. No riding equipment should be used on the climber, and no long scarves or loose capes should be worn.

When pricing climbers, you will probably find the best value from manufacturers in your own region. Shipping of large components accounts for a great portion of the cost, which is greater still when tariffs are added at national borders. So look for regional suppliers using chiefly local materials.

And make sure their equipment is scaled to the residential market. Don't waste your money on core logs or 6 x 6 timbers—unless you have a strong aesthetic preference for them and an unlimited budget. Those structures are built to take

A mini-climber, for small yards, patios
or basements

many years of extreme abuse in public areas. Your kids couldn't make a dent in them. Also, the more metal parts, the higher the price tag, so avoid heavy chains and sheet metal slides. Rope is well suited for backyard suspended equipment; polyethylene is ideal for slides.

If yard space is limited, think twice before installing a monolith smack in the center. You don't want to rule out other play options. What about sand and water play? What about a picnic table? Where can you toss a ball? A better option for small lots is a smaller, freestanding climber, particularly the portable types that can be carried indoors when the weather is bad. There are even models small enough for apartment patios, though their use is generally limited to preschoolers (see page 77).

The Right Components

Many manufacturers will let you customize your climber with the kind of slide, swings, decks, ropes and accessories that best suit your family. Take a look at all the options available in the catalogs. And if you really want to make an informed decision, take your kids on a series of field trips to different schoolyards and playgrounds. See which components challenge them the most, which pose hazards and which ones lack interest. Don't jump to conclusions—climb to them.

And once you've made an informed decision, don't be afraid to let your local school and parks board know how their equipment stacks up. The same safety considerations that apply to your backyard equipment can and should be extended to the public facilities in your area. If in your travels you come across hazardous equipment or play space design, make it known to the authorities. You might save a child from serious mishap.

...swings

While swings are without a doubt the most popular item on most playgrounds, they can also present the most conflicts and hazards. Appending them to a climbing structure can be a particularly risky proposition. Remember, not every backyard needs swings. Your kids might be safer and (without the battles over turns) happier using the more substantial swing sets in a nearby park or playground.

There are plenty of options for swingless backyard play structures. But if you do opt for swings, make an informed choice. Look for lightweight, flexible seats, not only because they give the best ride, but because hard, heavy ones cause greater injury on striking a child. (The most serious swing injuries are not to the swinger but to the standing child who is struck on the rebound after the swinger leaps off, or after pushing the swing himself.)

If you decide to install swings, your choice is between conventional (strap) swings or tire swings mounted horizontally on a swivel. The tire has the advantage

of providing a variety of swinging positions plus the social dimension of group
swinging. On the other hand, conventional swings can more easily be interchanged
with gym equipment, such as turning bars and rings.

Many of today's park and schoolyard designers are choosing the tire, but I
predict a swing back to the conventional style within the next few years. One of the
irreplaceable features of the conventional strap swing is the extremely relaxing,
almost hypnotic ride it affords. You can't get the same kind of satisfaction from
pumping a tire swing. Nor can you replace the escape value of solo swinging:

"We can think of no unit which so effectively and naturally insulates a child
from the rest of the group," writes a prominent American playground planner in a
design series published by the National Association for the Education of Young

Children. "A swing is really a safe place for a young child to watch without un-
wanted intrusion until he is ready to join others, and it is a good place for the tired
or the cross child to gain respite from the demands of group play."

Ideally, the entire swing unit should be physically isolated from other play
equipment. When installing swings in a climbing structure, follow these basic safety
rules:

— Make sure the swinging arc does not intersect active play areas or access
routes.

— Use adequate impact surface at least 6 feet beyond the outer limit of the arc;
leave an additional 12 feet of clearance between swings and slide exits or any other
active play areas.

— Leave 18 inches minimum clearance from supports and other swings,
measured at a point 33 inches above seat level; tire swings require a clearance of 24
inches from supports or other tires, measured from 59 inches above the ground.

Plastic slides are often safer and more fun than metal.

— Swings must be suspended no higher than 3 feet off the ground.

...slides

Who can blame kids for wanting to squeeze as much fun as they can out of a slide? The only control you have is in choosing a slide designed for safe multiposition use, and in applying a few basic rules to slide play. Beyond that, you can't effectively dictate how they should use their slide.

You can't force a five-year-old to sit up properly and slide down straight, nor can you prevent an eight-year-old from running up the slide and leaping down the other side. But through careful choice, a parent can limit dangerous experimentation. Listed below are points to consider when choosing a slide.

— Short wide slides provide the greatest variety of play for children younger than four, but a broad, long slide invites risky play.

— For kids older than four, the slide should be long, narrow and fairly steep, with a minimal slope of 2:1 (the slide bed is twice as long as it is high). A speed-up section of 1:1 part way down the slide adds a safe challenge.

— Wide slides for two or more children should be no longer than 12 feet.

— Entry space should be no wider than the width of the sliding surface, to prevent more children going down at once than the slide will safely accommodate.

— Straight slides need 3-inch safety edges from top to bottom; wave or spiral slides need 6 inches of safety edge.

— Slides over 5 feet long should have a run-off section (preferably parallel to the ground) at least 12 inches long, supported between 7 and 12 inches off the landing surface. This is the downfall of most wooden slides, which can't be contoured like metal or plastic to curb speed before landing. If you must use a straight slide, make sure the base is well off the ground to reduce landing impact on heels and backsides.

— Protective surface should cover at least 4 square feet of ground for landings. An additional 6 feet of empty play space should be left between the slide exit and other structures.

— A handrail 3 feet to 4 feet high should be mounted across the slide entry to give children a firm support before take-off and to promote single-file order on long slides. It is also handy in keeping bikes and skateboards off the slide.

— The design must allow young children to change their mind at the top of the slide. That's why slides attached to climber decks are preferable to most free-standing models. The old-style stepladder slide offers a narrow ledge (or worse, a sharp angle where the frame meets sheet metal) on which the child teeters before taking off. There is inadequate hand and foot support here for reticent sliders. A lineup of older and braver kids behind the tot will add to his anxiety. With a deck for him to sidestep onto, the odds of an accident or otherwise traumatic experience are greatly reduced.

— Plastic slides are most economical and practical in backyards, standing up to wear better than wood and staying cooler in summer than metal. If you choose metal, avoid burns by turning it to face north or northeast in sunny weather.

— Encourage kids to experiment safely by offering safe sliding alternatives, like the banister slide or fireman's pole. Banister slides, which are essentially two inclined parallel bars, provide an excellent range of bilateral coordination challenges — you can straddle the pair of bars or hug a single banister for a tipsy ride down, then shimmy back up on your stomach or climb with hands and feet. A fireman's pole offers a great upper-body workout and quite a thrill. (Provide ample landing surface!) Children will invent a dozen other uses for either of these alternative slides.

...ladders

For young children, ladders are extemely important in developing physical coordination as well as the mental exercise of motor planning. They learn to picture how they're going to get from A to B, then back to A again. Until they can manage the trip down as easily as the climb up, children should not be left without supervision on ladders. Generally, by age three, children are competent on low ones.

A well built horizontal ladder is invaluable in its own right for upper-body strength and coordination exercises. It can also form the skeleton of a very effective climbing–swinging–gym structure. (To support swings, trapeze bars, rings and the like, a horizontal ladder structure must be well balanced and anchored securely in the ground, preferably in cement footings. See page 87.)

Certain safety precautions apply to all ladders.

— Rather than using ladders as the main access to climbing structures, children younger than two should use slip-proof ramps with no openings between steps.

— Space between rungs should be uniform throughout a climbing structure: 9 to 10 inches for preschoolers; 12 to 14 inches for children older than five. Rungs less than 9 inches apart can cause head entrapment when a small child falls through.

— Positive angle of incline for rung ladders should be 75 to 90 degrees; for step ladders, no more than 75 degrees; for conventional steps, 35 degrees or less.

— To keep preschoolers off risky climbing equipment, the first step or rung should be at least 14 inches off the ground.

— Tire ladders pose a good challenge for children older than five, but too great a risk for preschoolers because of the irregular foot pattern required. Be sure the top tires in any climbing structure are secured from top and sides, to prevent them from tipping backward.

Decks add a vertical dimension and creative interest.

...rope

Only the strongest and most agile four-year-olds will rise to the challenge of rope climbing and swinging. A 1-inch polyethylene or polypropylene rope, anchored vertically to a climbing frame and knotted at regular intervals from top to bottom, offers a good introduction to hand-over-hand climbing. Until age seven or eight, children will need to support some of their weight on their feet, using the knots to propel upwards. Gradually, the challenge of climbing a straight unknotted rope will be met — a mammoth task of coordination and upper body strength.

(Unless we provide ropes, horizontal bars, ladders and the like, children will naturally concentrate on lower-body challenges. That is rather a shame, considering how much lower-body workout they get in the normal course of the day — just running down the street, riding their bikes and leaping over fences.)

Rope can be added to climbers in the form of nets, loop swings, rope ladders and pulleys. Non-nylon synthetics are the best all-purpose choice; nylon can burn skin while natural fibers, such as manila, are much heavier and prone to fraying, causing slivers.

...platforms and decks

Multitiered climbers are invaluable for creating vertical interest for older children and for keeping younger ones down where they belong. If a wide age range is involved, be sure the unit is designed to provide ample interest at each level. This will minimize frustration among little ones who are barred from all the really fun stuff that may be happening above their reach.

The best way to tier a climber is to let the kids create their own levels by incorporating loose parts, such as hollow blocks, cleated boards and ladders. If you have such resources on hand, be sure to buy or build a climber that accommodates them. It will increase play value of all your equipment tenfold.

The following safety points should be considered:

— Surfaces with a fall height of 3 feet or more should have guard rails to a height of 23 to 32 inches for preschoolers, and 27 to 40 inches for school-age children.

— Surfaces higher than 8 feet must be fully enclosed to a height of at least 3 feet. Make sure the railing offers no footholds for climbing. Slats in a crow's nest area must be vertical, not horizontal, to prevent over-the-top climbing.

— Use appropriate impact surface under equipment (see Chapter 2 for full details).

— There should be more than one way to get on and off a deck.

— Distance between stepped platforms used by preschoolers should be no greater than 12 inches, and up to 16 inches for children older than five unless steps between levels are provided.

— Watch out for gaps in platforms. Distances of between 4 and 9 inches are especially hazardous because of head entrapment.

Backyard Megaprojects

Let's not pretend this is going to be as easy as building a sawhorse. You'd better have some experience and a fairly complete toolbox to build a large play structure.

Your best bet may be to pool resources with friends and neighbors — among all of you there will likely be at least one good carpenter (with a basement tablesaw), one hobby draftsman, someone with a friend at the lumberyard, plus several sets of sturdy biceps. Older children can pitch in too, with sanding, nailing and finishing.

Your first decision is whether to build a fixed structure with sunken foundations, or a smaller freestanding model. There is debate over how big you can safely build without concrete footings. Many variables are involved: If the structure has large, wind-catching surfaces, it should have footings to keep from blowing over; if it rests on uneven ground, footings will lend stability; swing frames over 8 feet tall (for use by children older than four) should generally be anchored in concrete, especially if tire swings are attached.

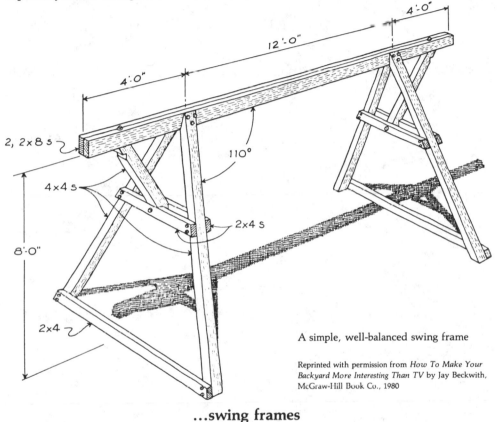

A simple, well-balanced swing frame

Reprinted with permission from *How To Make Your Backyard More Interesting Than TV* by Jay Beckwith, McGraw-Hill Book Co., 1980

...swing frames

Under the right conditions, it is possible to erect a stable, well-balanced frame to support a slide, horizontal ladder or swings for younger children without pouring concrete. Here are plans for a basic freestanding swing frame:

Materials
(fir timbers are recommended)

40 feet of 2 x 8, cut into two 20-foot lengths for horizontal crosspiece

46 feet of 2 x 4, cut into two 12-foot lengths for base horizontals and four 5-1/2-foot lengths for mid-leg braces

43 feet of 4 x 4, cut into four 9-foot lengths for legs and two 3-1/2-foot lengths for upper braces

85

SWING BEARINGS

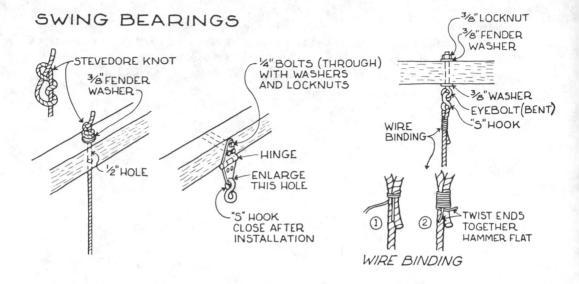

STEVEDORE KNOT

⅜" FENDER
WASHER

½" HOLE

¼" BOLTS (THROUGH)
WITH WASHERS
AND LOCKNUTS

HINGE

ENLARGE
THIS HOLE

"S" HOOK
CLOSE AFTER
INSTALLATION

⅜" LOCKNUT

⅜" FENDER
WASHER

⅜" WASHER
EYEBOLT (BENT)
"S" HOOK

WIRE
BINDING

① ②

TWIST ENDS
TOGETHER
HAMMER FLAT

WIRE BINDING

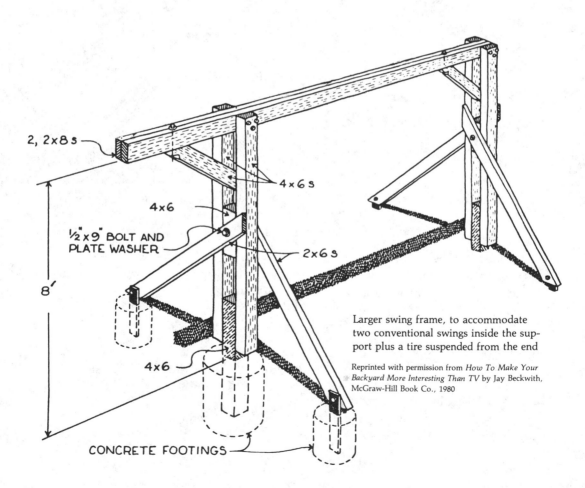

2, 2 x 8 s

4 x 6 s

4 x 6

½" x 9" BOLT AND
PLATE WASHER

2 x 6 s

8'

4 x 6

CONCRETE FOOTINGS

Larger swing frame, to accommodate
two conventional swings inside the support plus a tire suspended from the end

Reprinted with permission from *How To Make Your
Backyard More Interesting Than TV* by Jay Beckwith,
McGraw-Hill Book Co., 1980

With careful cutting and systematic rabbeting of joins for extra support, you'll find that this frame almost snaps together like a giant toy. Closely observe the 110 degree angulation of the legs to give a broadly balanced base. Lag bolts (1/2- x 9-inch for top fastenings) and plate washers should be used throughout; countersink to prevent children from scraping themselves on lower joins.

You can attach three conventional strap swings, spacing bearings 1 foot 8 inches apart, leaving a clearance of 21 inches between swings and supports or other swings. Use 3/8- to 1/2-inch nylon rope and one of the bearings on opposite page.

If you've watched older kids playing on a tire swing (especially when they're standing up, two or three kids to a tire) you'll understand why a freestanding frame will never suffice for this level of exertion. Here is a well-anchored frame that can support three conventional swings in the center plus a tire on one end, or alternately one tire in the middle and one on the end. Dimensions and materials are similar to the freestanding model, but in place of the large triangular supports this one is mounted on 4 x 6 verticals braced with 2 x 6s, all set in concrete.

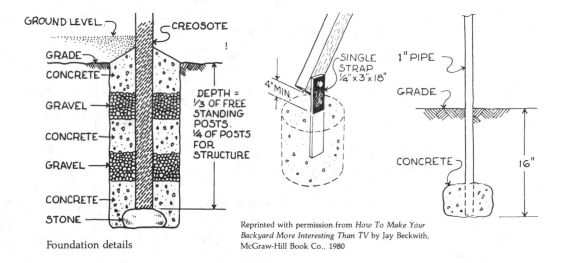

Foundation details

Reprinted with permission from *How To Make Your Backyard More Interesting Than TV* by Jay Beckwith, McGraw-Hill Book Co., 1980

...foundations for posts

The rule of thumb for swing frame (or climber) support posts is to set them into the ground at least 20 percent of their length, to a minimum depth of 24 inches. Freestanding posts should be sunk to a depth of 30 percent.

Layered concrete and gravel is most effective, built up on a stone base. Support timbers must be pressure treated to resist ground rot, with creosote on the sunken portion only. The top of the concrete footing should be tapered to drain away from the post, and buried beneath at least 6 inches of packed earth, not sand. (Sand can too easily erode, leaving the hazard of exposed concrete.)

...climbers

Let's start modestly, with an all-in-one toddler unit that every large family or small day-care center should have. (To qualify this point, I should add that I wouldn't build anything on such a small scale for my own two daughters because I'm sure by the time I completed it they'd be ready for a steeper challenge. However, if there were one or two more little Brooks waiting in the wings, I would seriously consider it. If I had fourteen, no question!)

What I like about this design (I've watched my own kids and dozens of others play on it at a community center near our home) is the two-foot square platform—larger than other mini-climbers on the market. It allows two kids to sit comfortably on top rather than tumble over one another to see who can get down the slide first. It also provides tea-party space for a couple of tiny grannies underneath.

The unit combines good safety features: well-spaced steps and handrails, proper slide rails and "lift-off" space at the slide exit to soften impact on heels and backsides. And because the slide and steps are fastened with carriage bolts and wing nuts, it easily disassembles for storage or moving to the basement for wintertime play.

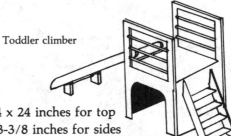

Toddler climber

Materials

Platform
— 1 piece 3/4-inch plywood cut 23-3/4 x 24 inches for top
— 2 pieces 3/4-inch ply cut 23-3/4 x 23-3/8 inches for sides
— 2 pieces 3/4-inch ply cut 23-1/2 x 23-3/8 inches for front/back

Rail
— four 20-inch pieces of fir or alder 2 x 2 for the verticals (drill three 3/4-inch holes 3-1/2 inches apart along the top 14 inches of each piece)
— two 2-foot pieces of same 2 x 2 for top rail (rabbet 5/8 inch to fit onto the tops of vertical rails)
— 12 feet of 3/4-inch hardwood dowel, cut into 6 pieces (insert into drilled holes in verticals rails)

Ladder
— 2 pieces 5/8-inch plywood cut 4-1/2 x 28 inches for sides (cut three 1/4-inch treads on each side, angled to match the 60 degree incline of the ladder)
— 3 pieces 3/4-inch plywood cut 4-1/2 x 15-3/4 inches for steps

Slide
— 1 piece 5/8-inch plywood cut 14 x 47-3/4 inches for base
— 2 pieces 5/8-inch plywood cut 3-1/2 x 47-3/4 inches for sides (round upper edges)

Construction

This unit gets its strength chiefly through the careful rabbeting of all support joints. Use standard 1/4-inch mitering on the four edges of the platform top and vertical edges of the platform's side pieces; the lower 6 inches of each vertical rail piece where they join the four corners of the platform; and the slide sides where they meet the base.

The only unorthodox rabbet is the 5/8-inch cut on the ends of both rail top pieces where they join the four verticals. All joints except the slide and ladder tops are secured with glue and countersunk wood screws.

The slide and ladder are fastened to the platform with carriage bolts and wing nuts, countersunk through small (4- to 5-inch) facings cut from scrap 3/4-inch plywood. Note angle cuts necessary to fit facings under slide top. Also, angle-cut two 4-inch wedges of plywood to support the slide base a few inches off the ground (to match 20-degree slide incline).

Every piece of this climber must be sanded velvet smooth, and finished with a tough varnish or exterior paint. Designer Craig Campbell of the Vancouver Community Workshop recommends marine enamel for a tough, bright finish that repels rain beautifully. For a more natural wood look, go for spar varnish rather than the usual urethane finish—the sun's ultraviolet rays cause urethane to quickly break down.

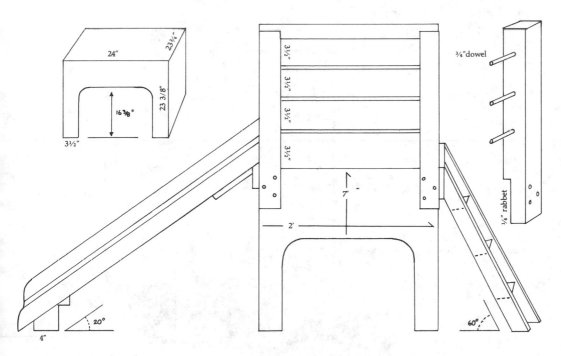

Details of the toddler climber

Designed by Craig Campbell,
Vancouver Community Workshop

Building a climber for older kids can be an adventure in its own right. First, look for a design that is easy enough to allow your young helpers to participate (under close supervision, naturally). This will make the prospect of playing on it all the more exciting for them, and will impart valuable lessons in construction techniques and safety.

Of course, once the kids get the hang of building their own play equipment, they will want to keep going. So be sure to choose an open-ended project. The one I've selected here is just that—it offers plenty of play opportunities as is, but retains a certain unfinished quality that inspires imagination. The deck can be closed over to lend intimacy, the lower timbers can accommodate walking boards or scrap lumber for "infill housing," and the upper beams can support climbing rope, swings or acrobatic equipment.

Materials:

> (use safely treated 2 x 6 or 2 x 8 fir unless otherwise indicated)
> Vertical Posts
> — six 8-foot timbers,
>   cut to 86-inches
> — two 10-foot timbers,
>   cut to 118 inches
> Horizontal Ring Beams
> — nine 8-foot timbers,
>   cut to 79 inches

Commando gym: see page 92
for details

Adapted from a design by John Boeschen, reprinted with permission from *Successful Playhouses* by John Boeschen, Structures Publishing Co., 1979

Commando Tower
- two 28 x 40 inch plywood boards
- one 28 x 72 inch plywood board
- one 28 x 50 inch plywood board
- 1-inch floor boards 32-1/4 inches long
  to cover 67-inch width

Ladder
- two 2 x 4s, cut 106-1/2 inches
- 11 hardwood dowels for rungs, 1 x 16 inches

Miscellaneous
- four creosoted foundation posts 4 x 6 or 4 x 8
  (to match the vertical posts used) 36 inches long
- three climbing boards 70 inches
- one horizontal bar 60 inches
- 1-inch hardwood dowel or pipe 5-1/2 feet
- three horizontal bars 6-1/2 feet
- 26 feet of 3/4-inch polypropylene rope
- soccer or cargo net about 4 feet 8 inches x 7 feet 3 inches
- four framing clips
- bolts, nuts, screws, nails and glue
- concrete for footings

Preliminary Work

Prepare the four foundation posts by cutting a tenon (a 10-inch long notch) on one end of each. The eight ring beams (which in pairs will provide horizontal support for the verticals) must be notched 1-1/4 inches deep by 4-1/2 inches wide to receive timbers (check appropriate width) 6 inches from the ends.

Drill the four pieces (two pairs of ring beams), which will support the three horizontal bars, by drilling through the two inside pieces and halfway through the outer members. These pieces also need to be notched in the middle to support the single crossbeam that carries one end of the floor boards. The ring beams are attached by lag screws between and inside of the verticals.

The other four ring beams are bolted together with blocking in between to form the last two crossbeams.

Into the ladder sides, drill 1-inch holes 8 inches apart. Cut small wedges out of the ends of the rungs, about 1-1/2 inches long, to form notches. Glue and nail the rungs into position and then drive somewhat larger wedges into the notches to lock the rungs in.

Erection

Connect the verticals to the foundation pieces and set about 24 inches deep into prepared footings (see page 87). Make sure posts are level. At 6-1/2-foot height,

Details of commando gym

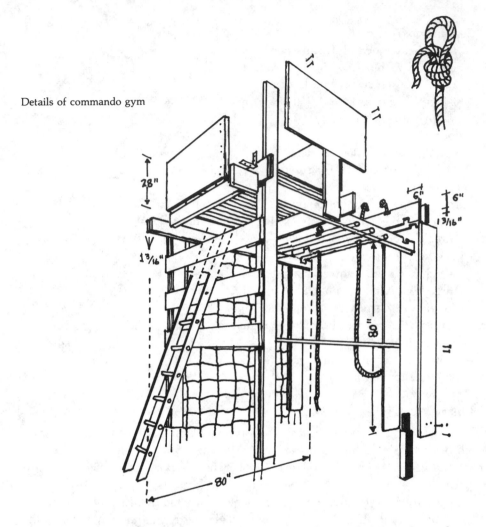

attach the horizontal ring beams with lag screws. The notches must be to the outside
of the vertical pieces.

The short posts for the railing and the railing itself are attached with screws.
Assemble the other side the same way.

Use metal framing clips to attach the ring beams to each other. Screw or nail
floor boards to the beams. Reinforce the post at the left of the railing with a piece of
scrap lumber.

The joint where parallel beams converge has a sandwich construction, with the
vertical members screwed to the horizontal boards. The parallel beam in each case is
held by an angle bracket attached with screws.

Fold net at the edges over strips, which are inserted between the verticals and
secured with screws. Attach lower horizontal bar with three carriage bolts at each
end. Protruding ends of the bolts should be sawed off and filed smooth.

Climbing and swinging rope ends should be double-knotted as shown and inserted into a shallow notch in the outside ring beams. Nail a piece of scrap lumber between the knots of the swing rope to prevent it from pulling out.

The ladder is stuck into the ground and fastened at the top to the protruding end of the ring beam with three screws. Finish by fastening the three horizontal boards on the ladder side with screws (these are for extra climbing, plus stability).

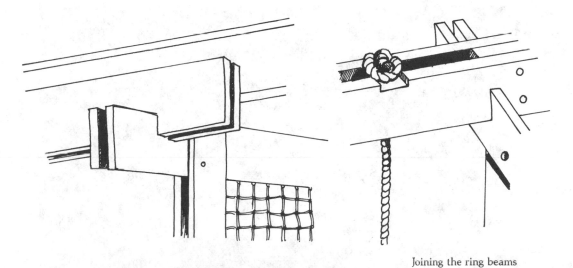

Joining the ring beams

Little hands make light work

Playhouses

Given the time, a little space and surprisingly simple materials, children will create their own private places. Whether it is a hideaway between two bushes or a refrigerator-sized cardboard box with a door hole, they will treasure it because it is theirs. I guarantee, you will not be depriving them by failing to provide a "proper" playhouse—carved shutters, lace curtains and all.

In playhouses, basic is best.

In fact, it would be a disservice to provide too much of a playhouse. If you're keen on building, a simple frame is ideal, either freestanding or appended (for convenience) to your climbing frame. Add a tarp or some lumber to the "Commando Tower" (see previous section) and you've got a fine elevated clubhouse. Or tuck a fort under your climber's deck. You don't get the same kind of remote privacy as you would in the bushes, but you do get practical advantages—like a proper roof over your head.

Just try to keep it to the bare bones. The fancier the design, the less valuable the results. Give your kids no more than walls and a ceiling. Let them construct the space.

Then let the kids tear it apart and construct it again. True constructive play is

best carried out in private, where children are their own bosses. No one tells them what the product should look like, or even if there should be one. This is precisely how the young mind and body are stretched by new experiences. Competence and a sense of responsibility are built through self-motivation, and through trial and error.

Framing the playhouse can certainly be a group project, involving parents, siblings and friends. This can add greatly to the social dimension of the playhouse, though it can also lead to trying conflicts. With major projects, your best recourse is the family council.

Remember to keep plans minimal. If you design the place right down to the floral wallpaper, you're only going to be annoyed to find someone's hand-painted cardboard shingles tacked all over it. Construction should be basic enough to allow for the constant transformations (and messes) inherent in a stimulating play environment.

Beyond the constructive and social benefits, a successful playhouse can be instrumental in stimulating the child's imagination — allowing him to improve on reality by creating his own little world. Some parents worry when they see children hanging around idly. They think of idle time as unproductive or wasteful. Far from unproductive, a place that encourages idle play and daydreaming is the best antidote to the anxieties of our achievement-oriented society. Kids should be allowed to waste time by the truckload in the luxury of their own private place.

Discuss needs and priorities before starting on a structure. How many children might want to play in it? How many activities will go on inside? Will a small

A playhouse can be many other
things, too.

Reprinted with permission from *Creative Playground
Information Kit 1*, by The Children's Environments
Advisory Service, Canada Mortgage and Housing
Corporation

playhouse accommodate all this? Will a large one impede other yard activities? Will
it be a fixed or movable unit? How much money can be spent on it? Is there another
pressing need in the backyard, like a support structure for a slide, or sheltered
storage, that can be met in the same design?

...basic construction tips:

1. Start with a scale model, using cardboard, pipe cleaners, popsicle sticks or
modelling clay. You'll be surprised how many new insights will come when you
have something concrete in front of you.

2. Let the design gel before acting on it. Expect it to change over the next few
days or weeks as planners dream up new twists and better angles.

3. Assemble the main materials before starting construction. This will help you
keep the budget in check and provide a variety of preparation jobs for junior
builders to do while the seniors get started on the frame. Much, if not all, of your
supplies can be scavenged to keep costs down. Scout construction sites for scraps
(ask before taking anything), solicit lumberyards for seconds, flooring shops for

samples and roll-ends, moving companies for packing crates, drums and cable companies or electrical contractors for wooden spools.

Scavenging needn't end once the structure is up. Keep an eye out for junked radio parts, old telephones, orphaned furniture, and dented pots and pans—new props are always required to keep playhouse drama fresh.

4. Keep safety in mind. If toddlers are around, keep them off elevated platforms by removing lower ladder rungs. Safety railings should be at least 3 feet high on any raised decks. There should be more than one way to get in and out. During construction, follow basic safety rules, beginning on page 21.

...building a frame

With a little help from their parents, a group of seven-and eight-year-old boys from Ottawa, Ontario, built this compact frame for under $30. One of the dads, an industrial designer, drew up the plans. The idea was to make the frame strong enough to withstand constant insertion and removal of nails as different variations rose and fell.

The frame doubles as a climber in its bare-bones form. Throw a sheet or tarp over it for temporary cover, or tack on cardboard shingles. For a proper finishing job, use exterior siding (check out the scrap bin at your neighborhood lumberyard), cut window holes and add a hinged door.

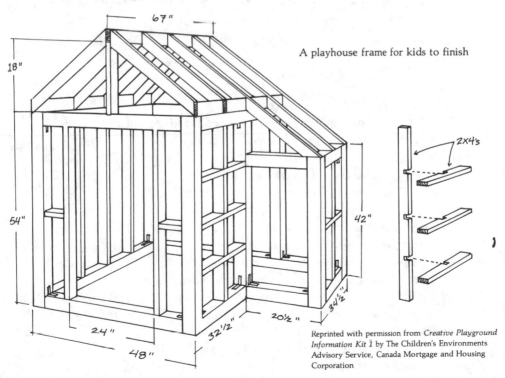

A playhouse frame for kids to finish

Reprinted with permission from *Creative Playground Information Kit 1* by The Children's Environments Advisory Service, Canada Mortgage and Housing Corporation

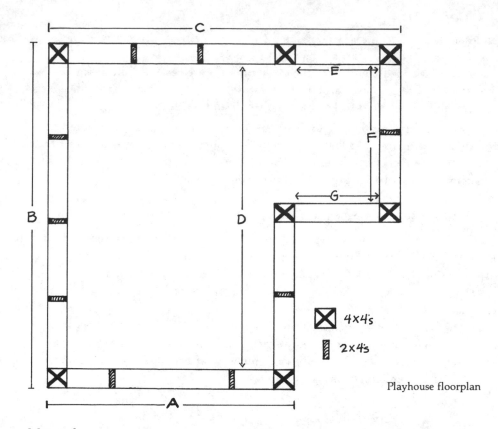

Playhouse floorplan

Materials

(use all safely treated fir or alder)

   4 x 4

   — 1 piece 61-1/2 inches for base of side C
   —3 pieces 60 inches long for base and top of B plus top of D
   —5 pieces 54 inches long for main vertical posts
   —3 pieces 41 inches long for base and top of A plus top of C
   —2 pieces 42 inches long for verticals of F
   —2 pieces 27-1/2 inches long for base and top of F
   —1 piece 29 inches long for base of D
   —3 pieces 17 inches long for base and top of G and top of E

   2 x 4 —buy twelve 8-foot strips and cut:

   a) for house: eight 47-inch verticals, one 35-inch vertical for side F and
      assorted shorter lengths for crosspieces (measure as you go)
   b) for the roof: one 67-inch king post, two 18-inch vertical supports, three
      48-inch rafters, seven 24-inch rafters and assorted shorter lengths for brac-
      ing

   3-1/2 x 3-1/2-inch metal angles at all 4 x 4 joints

   4-inch common nails; 6-inch lag screws

Construction:

You basically bang this frame together, one wall unit at a time. Secure 4 x 4 joints with metal angles, nail in the notched 2 x 4 verticals, cut and notch the 2 x 4 horizontals to fit, then glue and nail them into place to complete grid.

To frame the roof, use lags to join the king post to the 18-inch verticals and the verticals to the house frame across the center. To determine the angle of the rafters, hold one 24 inch piece in place (use a small step ladder inside the house) and mark the cutting lines on both ends with a pencil. Cut and use this rafter as a pattern for the others. (Note the three longer rafters on one end: they should be notched where they cross the 4 x 4 ceiling beam.) Rafters are 15 inches apart. They are secured at the base by 15-inch 2 x 4s, glued and nailed between rafters.

The "finished" product, ready for children

Buying a Playhouse

There are lots of playhouses on the market, but only a few good ones. The critical point, once again, is complexity. Most often, the fancier the playhouse, the lower its play value.

The best commercial playhouse is no more than a frame, to be built up and embellished in any number of ways. If it comes in kit form with a range of add-on options, so much the better. The kids should be able to decide on a daily basis what their structure is going to be—a space station, pirate ship, hospital or restaurant. A miniature townhouse complete with designer furniture and running water is always going to be a miniature townhouse.

You can add to the complexity of a playhouse through clever placement in your yard. Put it beside or (even better) on top of sand and you will enhance both the playhouse and the sandbox. Put it behind some trees, and you will find that the intense privacy stimulates new forms of imaginative play. Put it near an activity table or art cupboard, and the playhouse may become a science lab or art gallery.

A playhouse on sand
increases its play value.

Treehouses

There is no better place for a child to wile away a summer afternoon than in a tree. In fact, when I recall the long summer days of my childhood in a parched prairie town, I always picture myself comfortably ensconced along with a least one sister, two friends and a large thermos of Koolaid in the gently curving branches of our backyard elm.

Somehow it never occurred to us to build a treehouse there. We formed a tree club, held secret meetings—the works—sheltered only by a wall of leaves. Which is why I maintain you don't need lumber and nails to create a treehouse.

In any case, relatively few yards (and few trees) can accommodate a proper treehouse. If you want to build, first consider carefully whether you've got the right ingredients.

The tree should be well away from major structures and play equipment to prevent conflicts of interest and mishaps. (You don't want to entice a child onto the roof of your house or garage by placing a treehouse within leaping distance.) The tree must be mature—a thriving young one will literally burst the treehouse apart at the seams as it grows—and of a suitable type for support and climbing. The sturdiest trees are oak, eucalyptus, ash, pine and plane. Birch, beech, poplar, elm, cypress and most fruit trees are unsuitable due to weak limbs or susceptibility to wood rot.

The ideal support tree's trunk divides into three or more major branches between 6 and 8 feet from the ground. The branches should lie at a sufficiently broad angle to support at least three points of the structure's base on the same level.

If none of the trees in your yard measure up, you can get roughly the same effect by building an elevated deck around one or two trees. Use the ground for support (sink footings in concrete, as illustrated on page 87) and build a simple platform with 3-foot railings on all sides, with holes to accommodate the tree trunks. Access can be by rope or wooden step ladder.

Safety is a crucial consideration in treehouse construction, because you are adding height and often very awkward footing to the already risky combination of children and tools. It is a good idea for children under seven to remain on the ground until a safe structure is in place. All children must follow certain rules of treehouse play: No access during electrical storms; and no trailing scarves, capes or otherwise loose garments to be worn in the tree.

And remember to be nice to your tree. Use as few metal connectors as safe construction allows (lag screws are better than nails, which can easily dislodge with movement). Fasten rope loosely around limbs, looped rather than knotted, to prevent ringbarking. The kindest loop of all is backed with rubber stripping or a bike tire to minimize friction on the bark. And keep a tin of tree paint handy, to salve knife and saw wounds as you go.

Use the same logic as you would in playhouse construction. Keep to a basic frame, allowing the kids to add color, texture and props. But it is your responsibility

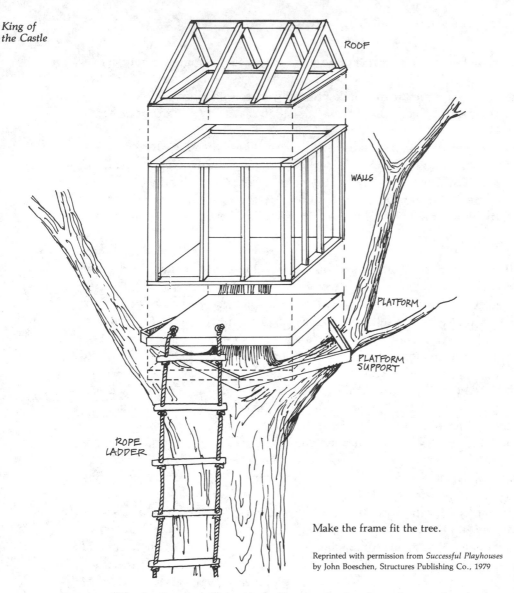

ROOF

WALLS

PLATFORM

PLATFORM
SUPPORT

ROPE
LADDER

Make the frame fit the tree.

Reprinted with permission from *Successful Playhouses*
by John Boeschen, Structures Publishing Co., 1979

to make the frame safe, with walls or guard rails at least 3 feet high and a well-
designed ladder or steps for safe access. Remove bottom rungs to keep toddlers out
of the tree.

With the right kind of tree, you can add bits and pieces to create an entire
climbing structure: knotted rope or nets can be used alongside or instead of ladders
for access; a swing or hammock can be strung below; a pulley is invaluable during
construction and after—to haul up snacks, toys and other supplies; and you can
keep a line of communication open with a simple walkie-talkie made of plastic funnels and a garden hose.

...building a treehouse

Because every tree is different, precise dimensions are not given for this model. To customize your own treehouse, take these basic measurements:
— distance between the three level points on which the platform will rest
— available height (clearance between the points and overhead branches or obstructions)
— clearance in length or width (note any other obstructions that might necessitate irregularities in the frame)
— distance from the ground (if steps or a ladder are to be built)

Materials
> 2 x 4s
> 2 x 3s
> 1 x 6 or 1 x 12 flooring planks
> 1/2-inch exterior plywood
> wood screws and/or lag screws, common nails, framing clips

Construction

Depending on the number of points, saw three or four support beams (2 x 4s) to fit the span between points. One at a time, screw them into the points using a level to make sure that the platform, which will rest on the beams, will be parallel to the ground.

Now get down from the tree and frame the platform. Use four 2 x 3s, measured to fit on top of the 2 x 4 base. Reinforce the platform corners with framing clips. Cut the flooring strips, glue and nail onto the frame.

Call in the troops to help hoist the platform up into the tree. Once up, make sure the platform rests securely on the 2 x 4 beams. Screw into place.

Frame the walls with 2 x 3s, and finish by screwing on 3-foot-tall plywood panels to the outside edge of the platform; secure upper corner joints with clips. Leave an entranceway of at least 12 inches in one side. The roof frame is a stripped-down version of the playhouse roof, also finished with plywood.

A regular or rope ladder (make your own, page 173) can be attached to the platform and anchored on the ground. Avoid nailing or screwing steps directly into the trunk.

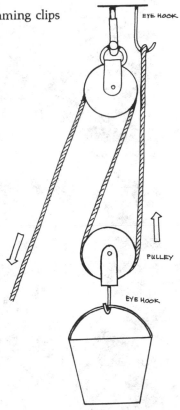

A pulley, to enhance treehouse play

CHAPTER 7

World's Best Tomato

Without a doubt, gardens are a lot of work. Soil preparation, daily watering and weeding, nightly slug patrol — with so many other interesting things going on in the yard, why bother?

Here's one good reason: Because you can't teach respect for nature. Respect grows in relation to the child's sense of *belonging* to nature. Alienation breeds disrespect. This I have seen firsthand in my own garden and at a nearby preschool where irreverent (or just plain thoughtless) attitudes toward plants — yanking flowers out of their beds, picking vegetables on a whim and then tossing them aside — change dramatically once children are given a chance to grow their own.

The simple miracle of growth closely observed for the first time, not to mention the painstaking attention required for successful gardening, breeds the kind of respect that harsh words and strict rules never can. This is true for toddlers and teenagers alike. Even adults can gain new regard for nature along with their children.

And here's another reason why you should cultivate a garden: Although you can't force kids to eat spinach, you will see them take a sudden interest in sampling what they've nurtured and harvested themselves. I can personally attest to this. My children believe sugar snaps are a treat equal to marshmallows. They eat them whole — right off the vine — inventing contests to see who can crunch the pod loudest, guessing how many peas are in each, and then counting the remaining blossoms on the stalks in flushed anticipation of next week's harvest.

The Plot

Think small, especially if this is your first year at gardening. Even if you have a large area at your disposal, limit your garden to a maximum width of 30 inches so

(a)

(b)

Planters make manageable gardens for children: wooden containers (a and b) need adequate drainage; old tires (c) retain the sun's heat.

the gardeners won't have to stand on one plant to reach another. You will also minimize the muddy shoe syndrome by designing the garden in such a way that most of the work can be done with feet firmly on border stones or grass.

If you have only a patio or balcony, don't despair. Lovely little gardens can be grown in wooden flower boxes, old whiskey barrels or any other well-drained containers. Put broken china or stones over drain holes before adding soil, to make sure the holes don't plug up.

Tire planters are favored by preschools. They're cheap (if not free) and really work well because the black rubber holds the day's heat right through the night. It's a good idea to broaden the top opening with a linoleum knife or hacksaw, to increase the planting surface. Be sure to cut drain holes in the bottom. You can even make these beasts pretty with any leftover outdoor paint (let the imagination loose on the tread patterns to make colorful planter borders).

In fact, many people with large yards prefer to work in planters rather than directly in the ground for a variety of reasons—they can keep plants well separated that way, perhaps using a large box for salad vegetables, one tire for herbs and another for flowers.

Whatever you use to contain your garden, make sure it is situated in a part of your yard that gets sun for at least half the day, and where water doesn't tend to collect in puddles. (If you have a drainage problem, mound the soil and dig gutters to divert the excess water.)

(c)

...soil preparation

Unless your plot has already produced for many summers and has been well composted over the winters, you and your team of gardeners will have to do some groundwork before you can expect results. Start as soon as the ground is frost free in early spring (in warmer climates, start as soon as the fall harvest is in, and continue to work the soil right through the winter).

First turn the soil over with a spade, spraying lightly with water if it is too packed. Pick out weeds, stones and foreign objects — but don't throw out any found treasures! Break up large chunks of earth with a rake, level the soil and leave it to breathe for at least two weeks. During this time add a well-composted manure (steer or chicken manure works well), digging it in and continuing to weed as you go.

If you do this conscientiously, you probably won't need to use fertilizers. But if you suspect your soil is poor (check it out by asking the best gardeners on your

With tools scaled to their size, children can take part in every aspect of gardening.

block) consult a garden shop or nursery for the best formula. Don't choose a fertilizer on a whim. There are hundreds on the shelf, and some will burn young plants, not to mention fingertips. No chemical fertilizers should be handled by children.

If you are planting in small containers, buy potting soil from a nursery to make sure your plants get the nutrients they need. Garden soil tends to pack tightly in pots, depriving roots of essential water, air and minerals.

Windowsill Gardening

Don't sit around waiting for spring thaw. It pays to get a headstart with protected indoor plantings, especially with half-hardy vegetables like tomatoes, peppers and green beans. Many types of flowers can also benefit from windowsill starts. Besides, there is nothing like a tray of seedlings sprouting in the morning sun to generate a heady anticipation of spring—the very best tonic for winter doldrums.

All kinds of containers are good for indoor sowing: egg cartons, sturdy cardboard trays, old kitchen pans—just be sure to punch small drain holes in them. Or, for under one dollar, you can buy proper seed flats at garden supply shops. You need just an inch of sterilized soil-based potting mix to start your seedlings. (If your children are younger than five, you'll probably have to act as supervising gardener, lending a hand when required. Older kids can certainly handle the entire process themselves, providing you've run through it at least once together.)

Dampen the soil by standing the whole container in a dish of water. You'll need to repeat this watering process daily, as loamy potting mixtures tend to dry up quickly. Level the soil with a piece of cardboard, then sprinkle seeds thinly (that's the tricky part) on the surface. Try using a wedge of paper to drop seeds onto the soil, spacing them no closer than a half-inch apart. Sift a little dry potting mix on top, just to cover the seeds. Enclose the tray in a plastic bag and set in a warm, dark place to germinate. Remove the plastic for an hour each day to circulate air. Keep

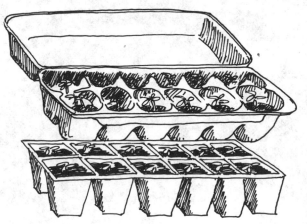

Daily progress can be observed and recorded from windowsill seedlings.

the soil moist, checking daily for shoots. Most seeds germinate within a week.

Once they've sprouted, remove the plastic and move the seed flats to a bright (not directly sunny) place. You can place them outside as long as all danger of frost is gone.

You will see very speedy growth from now on. As soon as your seedlings are tall enough to get your fingers around, you should start thinning them out. Take a look at the size of your plot, and consider the appetites of your gardeners. The most common mistake amateur gardeners make is overplanting.

If your plot is jammed with dozens of tomato seedlings, grit your teeth and pull out all but the sturdiest ten. That still leaves you with a safe margin for early wilters once they're in the ground. No junior gardener needs more than five healthy tomato plants—not unless he intends to stock the cellar with pizza sauce for the winter.

Most of these plants can go directly into the ground (weather permitting) once they have developed solid roots and stalks. But tomatoes and peppers should be moved to small pots first, where they will stay under sheltered conditions until they are at least four inches tall.

In cool climates, it's a good idea to 'harden off' these more vulnerable plants in preparation for outdoor life: Move the pots out for a few hours a day, increasing the time until the nights are sufficiently mild to allow transplanting. (Check the back of seed packets for specific temperatures.)

...windowsill reaping

The delayed gratification of gardening is more than a lot of young kids can wait for. Growing sprouts, on the other hand, is a nearly instant pleasure.

Kids can grow various types of delicate salad greens on the windowsill any time of the year. Mustard or watercress are great additions to salads and sandwiches. To start, line half an egg carton or any shallow dish with several layers of paper towels. Dampen them, sprinkle on the seeds, and cover with heavy brown paper. As soon as the seeds have sprouted, uncover and place in the sun. Water daily. Harvest with scissors when sprouts are at least two inches high. The whole process takes only a few days.

To sprout mung beans, peas, lentils or alfalfa, soak them in an unglazed clay or ceramic dish overnight. Drain the water, rinse the dish and replace the beans. Cover with a saucer and set in a warm place. Check daily, keeping damp but not soaked. Rinse if the sprouts smell sour. When they've grown proper tails, enjoy them raw in salad, cooked in chop suey or in a hearty stew. They also add a delectable crunch to peanut butter sandwiches.

...refrigerator raiding

If you are still waiting for nice weather and have window space to spare, raid the refrigerator for more gardening ideas. Most school-age kids can handle these projects on their own:

—Grow an avocado tree: Remove and wash the seed from a ripe avocado. (Please, eat the rest.) Prop it tip-up in a glass of water by poking three toothpicks around the lower bulbous portion, supporting the seed so that only the bottom is wet. Within a month a root will appear. When the root is three inches long, you can remove the toothpicks and transplant to a small pot, keeping the tip showing just above the surface of the soil. If your soil or potting mix is nutritious enough, an attractive tree will grow. (Snip the top to promote bushy growth.)

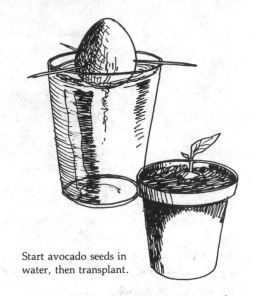

Start avocado seeds in water, then transplant.

—Start a hanging garden: Pilfer any kind of root vegetable from the refrigerator. Chop off most of the tip, leaving a chunk of about two to three inches to hang. Carefully carve a hollow in this chunk, using a slender knife or potato parer. Poke three toothpicks just below the cut edge, fasten string to the toothpicks and suspend from a curtain rod or hooks.

Fill each hollowed vegetable with water, and wait (a few days, perhaps weeks) for the strangest, possibly most ridiculous looking, window art you have ever seen. The hanging chunks of carrot, parsnip and rutabaga will soon be covered in mottled sprouts of all sizes, shapes and hues.

—Sprout a spud: Choose your favorite kind of potato, slice it into sections at least one inch thick, each with at least one eye. Bury the sections in a bowl full of damp sand, cover and set in a dark place until they sprout. Move to a sunny spot,

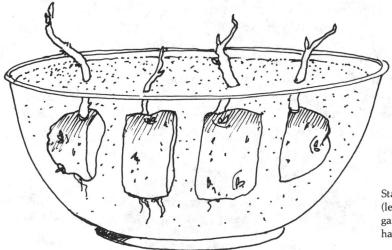

Start potatoes in sand (left), then transplant to garden for a fall spud harvest (next page).

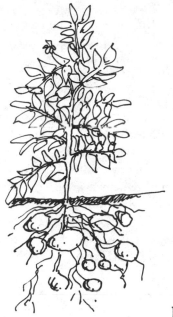

and when sprouts are at least two inches high, transfer them to the garden. With any luck the plants will flower within six weeks (in most climates, by mid-summer). When they do, it's a sign of potatoes forming; you should then limit watering to prevent rot. When the whole plant withers, dig up the spuds and enjoy.

How Sow?

You want to have the most productive, colorful, yummy garden on the block, right? Big ambitions, little plot. How are you going to manage it?

For starters, throw away all those gardening books that tell you to sow in neat rows. Think of your garden the way city planners think of high-density housing. The solution is the same, except that we don't call it 'infill'—we call it intercropping.

Bunch together the fast-growing plants with the slow growers: Radishes, small lettuce plants and any seedling crops, such as endive, coriander or garden cress, can be sown tightly around the larger cauliflower, cabbage, broccoli, turnip, parsnip, bulbing onion or artichoke plants. The little ones mature and are picked long before the big ones encroach on their soil.

Similarly, low-growing plants can be tucked under tall growers, as long as the lower ones don't need full sunlight. Sweet corn can be intercropped with trailing squash, cucumber, dwarf beans or seedling lettuce. Climbing plants on supports (cucumber, squash, green beans) and tall varieties of brussels sprouts combine nicely with seedling plants—including little lettuce varieties such as Tom Thumb butterhead and Little Gem romaine.

Seedling crops such as cress, coriander and many types of lettuce are ideal for impatient gardeners. They are sown thickly and harvested quickly, when the young plants are one to three inches tall. They are tender, tasty and often highly nutritious—seedling leaves have up to twice the vitamins of mature leaves in the same plant. They are also easy to sow, by scattering the seeds over a small soil block, then thinning the little shoots to 1 inch apart for cress and herbs, 4 inches for lettuce.

Seedling lettuce, of course, grows into mature lettuce, which can be picked (a few leaves at a time) right through the summer. No need to replant — just thin out the whole seedling patch to make room for some of your plants to mature.

...sow what?

If your family is as busy as most, you'll be looking for ways to streamline your garden, and get the most out of it for the least time invested. You might want to skip the seedling patches — who has time to snip and replant every few weeks? Pumpkins and many other memeber of the squash family are sometimes difficult to grow; you may have to help these big fellows along by rubbing stamens into pistils at just the right moment. And cabbages are a real pest — do you want to do battle all summer long with birds, slugs, snails, caterpillars, aphids, root flies and flea beetles?

Instead, limit your toil to a few no-fail varieties. Here is a sensible selection for novice gardeners: sunflowers, for great looks; climbing beans, for abundant harvest; and tomatoes — a labor of love.

Sunflowers are easy to grow, but their stems may need to be staked to support their huge, cheerful flowers.

Sunflowers produce seeds that can be saved for birds or roasted for snacks.

the seeds look like this.

Sunflowers:

These are an all-time favorite among young gardeners because they have such a positively happy look to them. Plant them as a border on the sunniest side of your garden, and within a few weeks you'll see them: Pretty maids all in a row.

There isn't much to sowing sunflowers. In early spring, poke the seeds about a half-inch into the ground, 2 inches apart. Cover loosely with soil, and water frequently. When seedlings appear, thin to at least 12 inches apart. (Use the strongest seedlings, transplanting if necessary.)

Sunflowers will grow to towering heights over the next few weeks and may need the support of stakes, especially if your yard is windy. After the flowers have withered, scrape off the black seeds and store some in a paper bag or covered tin for planting next spring. Keep some for the birds, and roast some for snacks.

Bean tepee:

Here's an idea that takes up little space but can produce a lot of food. In fact, you can do this in a flower box or large pot on a balcony, pulling up the old bean stalks and replanting in mid-summer for an extra harvest.

Buy packaged climbing bean seeds (dried cooking beans don't work) and sprout them indoors in early spring for a head start. While the seedlings are growing on your windowsill, construct your tepee — a very simple but ingenious little device that can also be used as part of an intercropping plan.

Plant three 6-inch sticks or bamboo shafts firmly into the soil, about 2 feet apart, lashing the tops together with garden twine to form the tepee frame. (The base can be narrower if you are planting in a pot.) When the seedlings are 3 inches tall, transplant two of them into the soil at the base of each stick (six plants in all).

113

As soon as the vines are tall enough to manipulate, start twisting them around the sticks. Pinch off the ends once they reach the top of the tepee. Weed and water often (daily in hot weather). Beans will appear within ten weeks, and the early ones will be tender enough to gobble up raw in salads.

For a large yield in limited space, vines can be trained around a bean tepee.

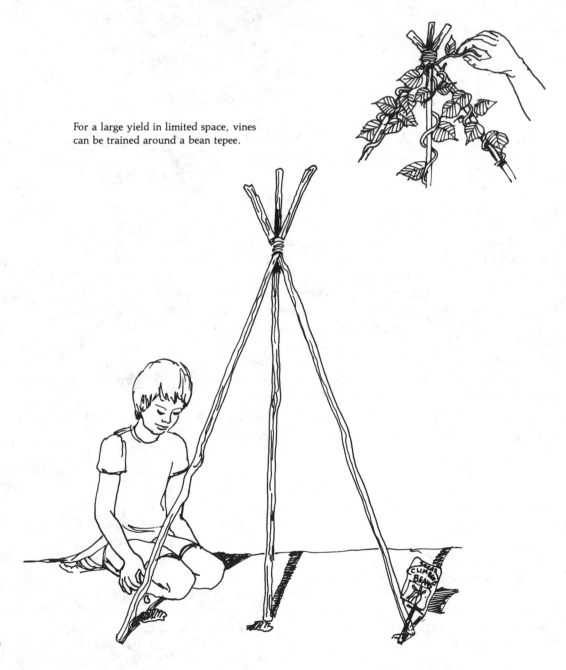

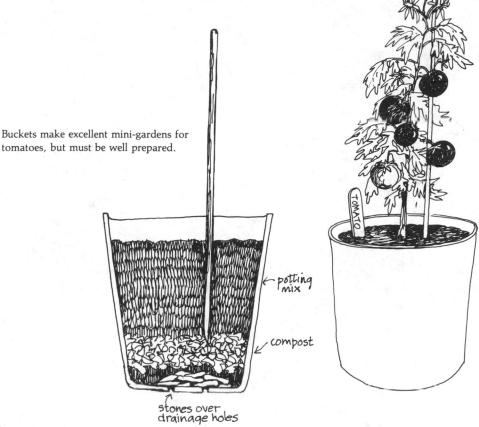

Buckets make excellent mini-gardens for tomatoes, but must be well prepared.

potting mix

compost

stones over drainage holes

I say, tomato:

Tomatoes are a bit difficult to grow properly, but more than any other garden crop, they are worth every moment of tender loving care that you are willing to devote to them. Homegrown tomatoes taste totally different from the store-bought variety, especially if you let them ripen in the sun and eat them immediately.

We usually start our seedlings on the windowsill at least a month before sowing time, growing three or four times more plants than we need for the garden. That way we can be very picky about which seedlings make it into the patch, picking only those with sturdy stalks and full foliage. The particular pleasure of growing your own from seed is the sweet tomato smell that even the delicate seedlings give off — it's enough to make your mouth water three months before the big red beauties land on your plate.

On the other hand, it is a lot safer to buy well started tomato plants from a nursery. You will probably end up with more fruit (they boost the young plants with special fertilizers to suit local soil) and a much lower casualty rate.

Either way, once the tomato plants have at least three sets of leaves, you can plant them outside, making sure they're in a sunny location, in warm soil, long past any threat of night frost. A bucket-sized pot is just as good as a garden for growing

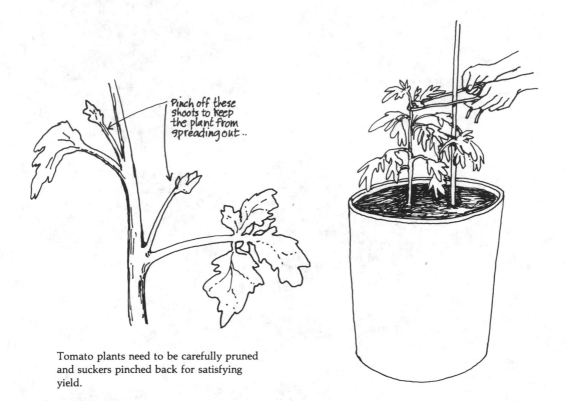

Pinch off these shoots to keep the plant from spreading out..

Tomato plants need to be carefully pruned and suckers pinched back for satisfying yield.

individual plants, as long as you use a good potting mix over a layer of compost or fertilizer, and stones or broken china over the drainage hole. If you are planting straight into the garden, mix in a little standard vegetable food.

Plant each seedling firmly, up to the first set of leaves. As they grow, watch closely for suckers (small shoots that grow out between the stem and larger branches). Pinch them off whenever you find them or you'll end up with a bushy plant whose many thin branches cannot support the weight of the developing tomatoes. It is better to force a few main branches to grow fat and strong.

Stake them up for support as the fruit appears. Pinch off the main stem when the plant reaches about 30 inches. Water often, wetting the soil around the base rather than the leaves.

The plants will start producing tomatoes within two months of planting outside, and may continue into early fall. As soon as frost threatens, pick any remaining fruit (even the green ones) and let them ripen in a paper bag or on the windowsill. You can pickle the green ones in a vinegar brine, or sweeten and bake them into a pie as you would rhubarb—the taste is quite similar.

...tools & rules

Every gardener should have these tools: spade, garden fork, rake, trowel and hoe (a small onion hoe is much handier for weeding than the larger types). Most of these can be improvised from household utensils: A large spoon or ladle can double as a trowel; any small sturdy shovel can be used as a spade. But certain minor investments will prove their worth: A long-necked watering can with a fine-holed detachable nozzle is essential for seedlings, which require a very light spray. Detach the nozzle for mature plants, which should be watered directly on the soil base rather than completely soaked by a hose or sprinkler.

In fact, sprinklers should be avoided entirely in small-scale gardening. They tend to water leaves more than roots (causing sunburn in hot climates) and they waste a lot of water on surrounding soil, which only encourages healthy weeds. The most economical method of watering is to sink a porous (unglazed) clay pot into the soil very near the base of each large plant, keeping it topped up with water. The water will seep slowly through to the roots, and you can easily see when the plant is thirsty.

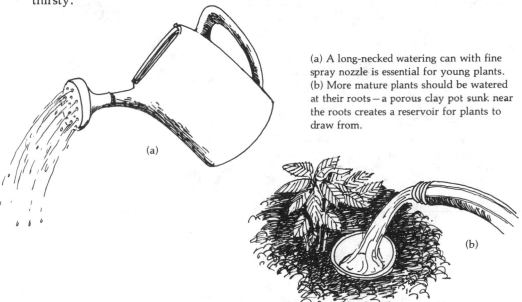

(a) A long-necked watering can with fine spray nozzle is essential for young plants. (b) More mature plants should be watered at their roots—a porous clay pot sunk near the roots creates a reservoir for plants to draw from.

The basic gardening rules, like all matters of discipline, should be kept to a minimum but observed to the letter. Too many rules ruin the fun; too few can encourage serious accidents. Following are some good gardening rules:

1. Take out only those tools you will need for the task at hand.

2. Put them safely away when you are finished. (If very young children are underfoot, constant supervision will be required. Safe storage should be carefully designed to give access to older kids while keeping little hands off.)

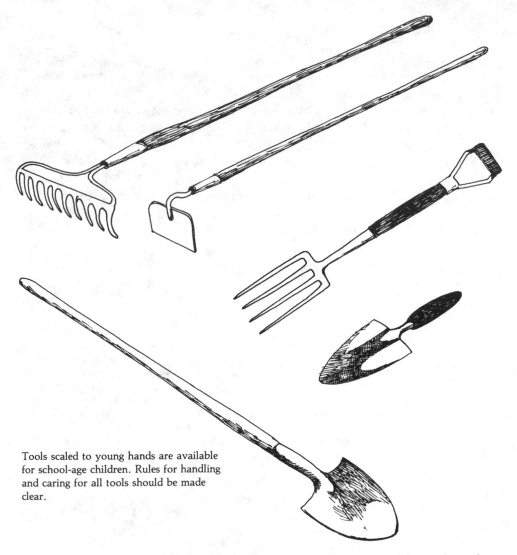

Tools scaled to young hands are available
for school-age children. Rules for handling
and caring for all tools should be made
clear.

3. Do not leave hoes or rakes with teeth or blades upward. Always lean them
against a wall.

4. No running or hitting with tools, and no throwing or swinging tools.

5. Whenever possible, look for organic solutions to pest or disease problems.
Snails and slugs, for example, can easily be corralled and discarded without using
commercial poisons. Simply offer them a shady spot on hot days by putting a damp
piece of cardboard or a soaked wooden plank in one corner of the garden; wait for
them to slither under, then collect and discard them.

Many caterpillars can also be manually removed from your garden before they
eat up your entire lettuce patch. (If you'd like to keep one or two for observation, see
page 147.)

When the survival of your garden is at stake, you may have to use pesticides or antifungal sprays. If your neighborhood garden shop doesn't have an organic option, shop around. Not only will the birds, pets and babies around your yard be protected from unnecessary exposure to toxic chemicals, but you will also feel safer about eating the vegetables.

6. Establish a rotational duty chart so that the children (you may include neighbors) know clearly who is responsible for watering, weeding and cleanup. Don't leave toddlers out of the action; they enjoy routine responsibilities and can perform surprisingly well when made to feel needed. Keep adult intervention to a minimum. The gardeners themselves will quickly learn to settle disputes over fair work and fair play in a communal garden.

7. Make the whole crew aware of plant poisoning hazards:

— Get to know which plants in your yard and your neighbors' yards are dangerous. (See Appendix II, page 173.)

— Store seeds and bulbs away from young children.

— Positively identify a plant (including wild ones) before touching or eating.

— Do not attempt to make herbal remedies, teas and the like unless you are expertly qualified to do so.

— Always wear long pants and sleeves, tall socks, enclosed shoes, and gardening gloves when pruning thick foliage.

CHAPTER 8

Sandicrafts

S and can be a major source of creative pleasure for children, and a major head-ache for parents. Sand has the unpleasant habit of getting everywhere. Add water and the inevitable result is wet kids, not to mention messy kids, which leads to messy floors and chronic ring-around-the-tub. Add pets, birds and bugs to this picture and you're looking at a health risk. In short, you can't just put the stuff in your backyard and forget about it.

But if you are willing to invest a little time to think through the problem, and some muscle power to build (or cash to buy) the right equipment, you will unquestionably find that your investment pays off handsomely. Nothing absorbs a child's attention and energy like sand play.

The sandbox is one of the only elements in the standard playground that kids can influence and change according to their own ideas, making it one of the very

best investments in complex play equipment. From a developmental viewpoint, sand stimulates experimental and exploratory behavior. Sensually, it's a goldmine. All it takes is careful planning to successfully incorporate sand and water play into your yard.

Foresee the Mess

Place the sandbox and water outlet where cleanup is easiest. You can't expect sand to stay in the box: Transporting it across the yard via dumptruck, or making cakes on a nearby work surface is half the fun. Such fun ought to be encouraged—within reasonable limits.

Make it clear to your children what those limits are. Sand should never be thrown and should be kept off grass, to save on mower blades. You might want to specify trucking routes around the patio, and establish dumping sites within easy sweeping distance of the sandbox.

Truck drivers and bakers should be expected to clean up after themselves—a task which needn't be too arduous in a well-designed play space. The tidiest design I've seen is a sunken sandbox, built into the patio or deck, allowing the child to simply sweep sand back into the pit at the end of the day. But a raised box will pose no problem if whisk brooms and dustpans are handy.

Storage should be provided for sand toys. Most of us appreciate the contribution that an organized storage and retrieval system makes to indoor play—not only to the physical condition of the playroom, but to the quality of the children's activity there. When a child enters a room littered with model car parts, bits of Legos and odd puzzle pieces, the chances that he will settle down and play in a concentrated fashion are slim. He is more likely to kick through the clutter, pick something up, start something else, get impatient looking for a lost bit, and leave in search of easier gratification elsewhere.

The scenario is the same outdoors, especially when it comes to sand and water play because that's where kids tend to collect the most tools, toys and junk. Though it is tempting to toss everything into the sandbox at night, the certain result is that the whole area eventually takes on the appeal of a garbage dump. Even the most enthusiastic freeway builder may be deterred from her plans by the prospect of having to first clear away the clutter.

The solution can be simple. Keep a few plastic milk crates or any other stacking containers nearby, possibly assigning one to each child or to each activity. (Pails and shovels here, cars here, baking pans here, and so on.) If you are building or renovating a deck, consider bench seats that open into toy chests.

The Sand Dump

I have seen people dump a load of clean play sand into a remote corner of their yards and let their kids loose in it. Occasionally this system (or lack of one) works extremely well. It helps if the property is sloped to allow natural runoff; otherwise a leach pipe or a foundation of clay bricks would be necessary. Wet, stagnant sand is both unappealing and unsanitary.

Because it would be difficult to cover, the sand 'dump' is not recommended if undisciplined dogs or cats are about. Nor is it a good idea to locate the sand where tree or bird droppings are bound to be a problem. Even without these little treasures, you are going to spend a good part of your summer raking the sand. So choose a location that will minimize the task.

The best dump I've seen is in a friend's backyard on the slopes of West Vancouver's Hollyburn Mountain. This family had the natural advantage of having an underground spring nearby, which they diverted to one side of their property to create a bubbling freshwater spring that runs down the length of the yard and drains to a storm sewer in the back alley.

Early each spring my friends truck in 6 cubic yards of washed construction sand, at about $12 a yard. That's their entire outdoor play budget for the summer, and it provides four or five months of constructive activity: Armed with shovels and scavenged materials (lumber scraps, plumbing pipes, etc.) the children build dams, shipping canals, locks, bridges, tunnels and waterfalls. Boats are sailed downstream, vast castles built on the banks, and gooey cakes served on wooden trays.

If your landscaping allows it, provide your children with an unstructured sand and water area, and you will keep them occupied for days on end.

The Best Boxes

Few backyards are large enough (or well enough endowed by nature) to accommodate such a lovely dump. Most of us are far better off with a box —a relatively small one at that.

If yard space is tight, a store-bought model may be your best bet. (If it's *really* tight, see Chapter 3 for ideas on adapting sand and water play to small patios.) Look for a resilient polyethylene or polypropylene frame—light enough to move under the porch in winter and tough enough to take a few kicks. Little Tykes has an excellent line of moderately priced sandboxes with molded plastic lids that double as water-play units.

Even if space is not a problem, resist building the giant sandbox variety, which are usually designed to combine both the play and impact functions of sand. (The box or sand pit is positioned around climbing and gym equipment.) Such a setup only sounds like a practical idea. In fact, you will ruin the quiet, creative aspects of sand play by bringing climbing equipment into the area. The idea invites both conflicts and accidents. It also ignores the material difference between round-particle

A sand-and-water unit from Little
Tykes, offering enough options to occupy several kids at once

impact sand and finer play sand. And it can create a hygiene problem because it's
unlikely that you'll be able to keep such a large sand area covered.

A well designed sandbox deserves separate consideration from the climbing,
swinging and jumping components in your yard. The dimensions of the sandbox are
not as important as the quality and depth of the sand—10 inches is the ideal
minimum. The sand should be a balanced mixture of particle sizes, no coarser than
1/16 of an inch, should resemble seaside sand, and be just as easy to pack and shape.
It should be free of clay, silt, oxides, iron and other contaminants.

It is not crucial for every kid on the block to fit into your sandbox. In fact, a
successful sandbox may accommodate no children at all. A design favored in Britain
and Europe (where urban space is at a premium) treats the sandbox as a mere container from which sand is taken for use in the surrounding play area. Wide wooden
edging around the box can be used for seating or to run trucks along. A common addition to the English sandbox is the cake table—a small working surface inside or
near the box on which children can master their fine sandiworks.

A simple alternative is a good-sized corner seat that can double as a work surface. Two of these would be sufficient for a box 5 feet by 5 feet or smaller. Larger
sandboxes can accommodate one seat in each corner.

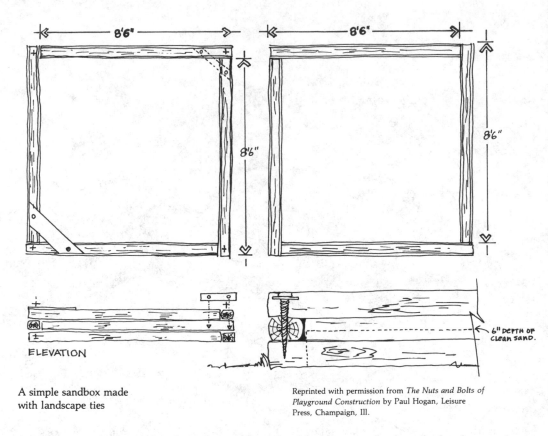

ELEVATION

A simple sandbox made
with landscape ties

Reprinted with permission from *The Nuts and Bolts of
Playground Construction* by Paul Hogan, Leisure
Press, Champaign, Ill.

Here is a basic timber box that you can build using standard uncut landscape
ties. The finished sandbox will be 8-1/2 feet square—a generous family-sized box
that will comfortably accommodate three or more children plus toys. (Be sure to
buy ties preserved with pressure-treated saline solution, the least toxic preservative.
Avoid creosote.)

Materials

    12 landscape ties (non-toxic preservative)
    four 3/8 x 10 inch lag bolts
    four 1/2 x 1-1/2 inch fender washers (ext. 0)
    four 30-inch pre-cut metal cross ties, bored at each end
    treated timber or plywood for seats, cut to desired size

Construction

    Stack the twelve ties as shown. Drill or chisel out countersunk holes 1-1/2 inch
round x 3/4 inch deep. Install lag bolts and washers to align the four corners. Brace
the corners from below with metal cross ties, and from above with corner seats

made of pressure-treated timbers or plywood pieces (sand well and finish with at least three coats of outdoor paint or varnish). Cross pieces should be fixed firmly in place with two-inch wood screws.

Some families will want to feature a large, relatively permanent sand play area in their yard. A well drained sand pit, with retaining walls of stone or timber, can provide tremendous play value as well as an attractive addition to backyard landscaping. Below are two sand pit designs, utilizing layers of crushed stone in varied sizes.

Portable cake tables
add working surfaces

Keep It Covered

There are dozens of ways to cover a sandbox: Put hook-and-eye fasteners at four corners of an oilcloth tarp; screw handles onto a well sanded and finished piece of plywood; or construct a simple box-type lid that converts the sandbox to a picnic table or plant stand when closed. To cover a sand pit, secure a tarp over the retaining walls. But whatever design you choose, make sure it effectively keeps rain and foreign bodies out while allowing air to circulate for natural sanitation.

Unless you want to be called into action each time your children start or finish their sand play, keep the cover as light and manageable as possible. I have seen very impressive designs (one uses wooden slats on a sprung support frame; another has tarps suspended over the box with a rope pulley system) which prove unmanageable over time, even for the adults who built them. Fancy systems like these usually have a fatal flaw that eventually leads to open sandboxes and contaminated sand. (It doesn't take much—one stray cat can make several toddlers sick.)

Because sand play is a favorite pastime of the very young—mine started as soon as they were old enough to sit up—sandbox hygiene is a serious matter. Tiny children will put sand in their mouths; or, at the very least, sandy fingers will find their way into food. You can treat this casually when it happens during occasional visits to the beach. But if the child is playing in an unclean backyard sandbox on a daily basis, you're looking at a hefty intake of bacteria.

Your first precaution is in choosing well washed sand. Construction suppliers sell sterilized sand in bags, at a premium. A more economical choice is buying washed sand in bulk, and sanitizing it yourself with a chloride solution:

— Mix 1/8 cup fluid chloride of lime in 3 quarts of water for each 2 cubic yards of sand (a 6-foot-square box holds between 1 and 2 cubic yards);
— Sprinkle mixture over sand using a watering can, then hose it lightly to ensure penetration, without waterlogging;
— Turn sand over with a shovel, and let it breathe for a day before children can resume play;
— Periodically turn and rake sand throughout the season, removing debris.

Multi-tiered, covered sandboxes

Even if you start with sterilized sand, a heavily used sandbox should be disinfected at least once a season in the same fashion. The sand should be periodically turned over and raked, to let in air, and left uncovered to dry in the sun. (Place the box where it catches sun in the morning but is at least partially shaded in the afternoon. There is nothing more dizzying than spending a whole summer afternoon in a sun-baked sandbox. Children will do that, unaware of the heat hazard — until it's too late.)

And Keep It Wet

The play value of sand increases tenfold with the addition of water. Children instinctively know this, and if you don't supply the means, they will certainly figure out their own way — possibly at the expense of your deck furniture and lawn — to bring the two together.

When planning for sand-and-water play, you must first tackle the drainage problem. Bring a hose into a sealed sandbox and within seconds you've got a murky pond on your hands. Yet it's a shame to outlaw the hose — by far the most versatile backyard water source. Instead, adapt your sandbox for water play.

If you are building a sandbox in a suitably derelict corner of the yard, frame it with timbers but don't put in a bottom. (The landscape tie design is a good example.) Install drain tile or a leach pipe flush

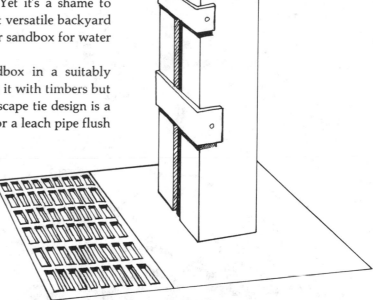

You don't have to be a plumber to install an easy-access water supply in the backyard. An automatic shut-off tap eases the drainage problem.

Reprinted with permission from *Creative Playground Information Kit 2* by The Children's Environments Advisory Service, Canada Mortgage and Housing Corporation

with the earth, under the sand. If you have natural runoff, a layer of clay brick will suffice. If you have already purchased a sealed box, place it where leakage will do the least harm, and punch a few small holes in the bottom. Either way, leave the cover off for a portion of every sunny day to make sure the sand dries thoroughly.

Any backyard water outlet can be enhanced for children by adding some simple plumbing hardware. Bring the pipe up to the height of about 3-1/2 feet, mount it on a treated 6 x 6-inch wood post that is set into the ground to a depth of at least 3 feet, and attach an automatic shut-off tap. If you don't have a handy underground source, this setup can be adapted to fit a garden hose by adding an elbow to the pipe at the base of the post. Dig a catch basin under the tap, with drain pipe leading to a storm sewer, and cover with a metal grill.

Kompan Playscapes makes a state-of-the-art backyard tap called the Water Hen — a delightful device. The Water Hen is a portable wooden stand topped with a brightly colored hen's head, which acts as a protective plate over the automatic shut-off tap to protect children from falls against the hardware. Mounted on a slatted drain board, the whole thing is easily moved to different parts of the yard as the action shifts, and just as easily stashed in the garage for the winter.

In fact, Kompan (based in Denmark with United States headquarters in Windsor Locks, Connecticut) makes a complete line of perfectly delightful sand and water equipment. They are small on sandboxes, but big on cake tables, splashing tables, bucket tables and other sand play equipment. This is obviously the direction sand

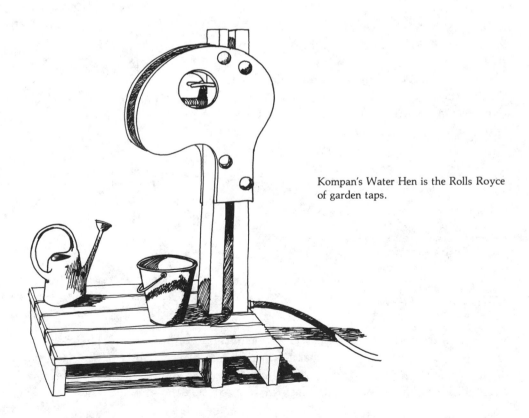

Kompan's Water Hen is the Rolls Royce of garden taps.

A portable, sturdy water bucket with pump is cheap, practical, and builds biceps.

play is taking in Europe, with the forward-thinking Kompan Inc. leading the pack.

On the other hand, there is nothing wrong with making your kids work for their water. A basic pump system that is portable and sturdy is illustrated below.

Construction

Buy or scavenge a wooden whiskey barrel, preferably one with metal bands that can be tightened as the wood ages. The half-barrels commonly sold as deck planters are ideal because they're small enough to roll into place, and low enough for a small child to reach.

First, clean it thoroughly inside and out, checking for splinters or rough edges. Waterproof the inside by sealing with three coats of fiberglass resin. Similarly treat a half-circle piece of 1-inch plywood, measured to fit over half the barrel's rim. Drill a hole in the center of the plywood, just large enough to snugly fit the shaft of a standard metal hand pump. Mount the pump on the plywood, and firmly screw the top onto the barrel. Place the barrel near sand play area, and fill with water.

Once you've installed an easy-access water outlet, you will be tempted to take the next step and install a shower. All you have to do is raise the piping, and fix it to a handy wall or fencepost. Plumbing experts may go the whole route to hot and cold pipes, but for most families, the basic cold drip will do the job. Besides solving the sandy house syndrome, an outdoor shower is a cool place on hot days.

And on to the next step—a stream. This will take more work, because you have to create a bed of stones, clay bricks or sand, which will wash away and have to be replaced periodically. A successful stream also relies upon suitable ground contour and drainage. Stagnant pools lead to coliform problems.

Here is a deluxe playstream design from the files of landscape architect Cornelia Hahn Oberlander:

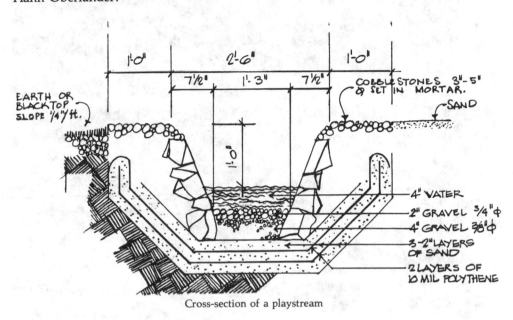

Cross-section of a playstream

Once you've laid the groundwork, the mechanics are simple. Use a tap or pump at the top, add clay piping or metal troughs to create waterfalls, and dig hollows downsteam to create ponds. If children under age four are about, water should be no deeper than six inches.

Backyard Scientist

Because everything is new and exciting to them, preschool children are natural scientists. They don't need prodding to go out and explore. They don't require fancy equipment — just their own five senses.

But they do need your support and encouragement, or they will soon learn that nature is far too large and scary for them to tamper with. They need to have the world brought down to their level. In the course of their very serious pursuits, a good deal of attention and patience is required — of their parents, and of themselves. No one said it was easy to discover the world.

Kids can get pretty cocky about the scope of their worldly knowledge by the time they hit first grade. Is it something about our culture (TV? the school system? too much sugar on the Sugar Pops?) that often turns innocent, curious young people into armchair know-it-alls? In any case, concerned parents ought to rise to the challenge by bringing a little wide-eyed wonder back into their children's lives, and into their own.

The best strategy is to open your own eyes wide to the wonder all around, and to share your enthusiasm with your children. This can certainly be done whenever you're together, wherever you are — answering their 'whys' with stimulating 'becauses,' bringing attention to the great and tiny physical changes on all sides.

But to sustain interest in nature and science, especially beyond the primary grades, it pays to get organized. And again, what better place than your backyard — an open-air laboratory just waiting to be staffed by scientists.

Equipping the Lab

All you need is a work area with a table and shelf space, some stimulating resource material from your public library, plus a few basic pieces of equipment.

Hand lens for magnifying: small pocket models are fine for school-age children; younger ones with unsteady hands will prefer a large lens supported on a tripod, about 12 inches tall. Once children demonstrate a serious interest, you may want to invest in a microscope, or move on to a telescope.

Collection cases: egg cartons, shoe boxes, plastic or metal containers with lids, empty milk cartons, ice trays, foil pie plates and bottles with corks

Mounting materials: sheets of stiff cardboard cut from boxes, styrofoam, bristol board and a scrap book

Classifying materials: paper or gummed labels, pens and pencils, coloring supplies and paints for embellishment

Tools and miscellany: blunt-ended scissors, spoons, garden trowel, sieve, string or thread, paper clips, tape, and clear liquid glue that can be applied with an eye dropper or spray bottle.

Measuring equipment: cups and larger plastic containers should be translucent, have handles and be calibrated clearly with raised lines in metric and English measure; a plastic funnel set; and assorted bowls and basins.

Scales: not absolutely essential but always interesting. Look for either the rocker type with hanging basins on both sides (good for comparing two different substances) or simple scales with only one basin and a set of weights. Buy plastic scales to keep the price under $25.

Magnifying equipment is a must, ranging from small hand lenses to a tripod for unsteady observers.

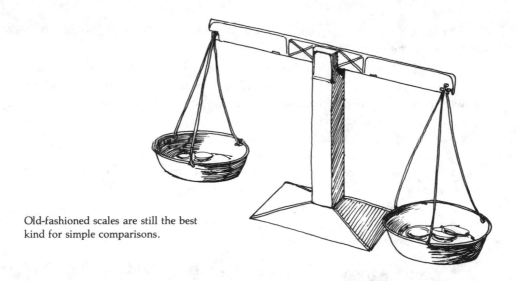

Old-fashioned scales are still the best
kind for simple comparisons.

...the collector

Once your backyard science center is in place, you'll be amazed how quickly
the kids take to the task of collecting and classifying things. This is the basic art of
investigation: Interesting objects are found, examined, compared, measured and
stored for future reference. In this way children not only learn a great deal about the
objects, but learn crucial organizational skills as well.

There are times, however, when they will want to simply mess around with the
equipment, testing their 'lab skills' with random samples of yard debris. Often, this
is the best option available to younger siblings who would love to get into the act
but don't have the patience or attention span to embark on a serious project. Resist
bringing advice or structure to bear at times like these. They may or may not be on
the brink of some earth-shattering discovery. Give them the benefit of the doubt.

If your children appear to be at a loss for ideas, or if they approach you for sug-
gestions, start by sitting down together with a good book on the natural sciences.
For children younger than ten, simple picture books are often the most stimulating.
If questions can't be answered to their satisfaction, refer to an encyclopedia or field
guide. Make this a habit and you will impart to your children one of the most enduring lessons of science—the ability to thoroughly research a subject.

Children should also be encouraged to keep their eyes open for lab specimens
beyond the back fence. The sign of a true junior scientist is a pocket bulging with
found treasures en route to school or piano lessons.

Give them some starter collection ideas, such as the following:

— Soil Types. Poke around your own garden, a nearby playing field, stream
bed or wooded area for a wide range of samples: sand, clay, gravel, loamy soil (mixture of sand and clay), and humus (a dark, loose mix of decayed plant and animal
material). Test each for water retention. Do weight-to-volume comparisons. In a

long-range experiment, try planting different seeds or seedlings in the various soils and observe the results.

— Grass Types. Did you know that rice, corn, wheat, rye, barley and oats are varieties of grass? With a hand lens, children can examine the wild and cultivated growth in and around the yard, looking for the five characteristics of grass:

1. stems with solid joints;
2. one leaf at each joint;
3. each leaf pointing in the opposite direction from the one below;
4. the sheath of each leaf wrapping aound the stem and the thin blade extending outward;
5. tiny flowers growing on fine branches in the mature stage.

Specimens may be dried and mounted in the same manner as flowers (see page 140).

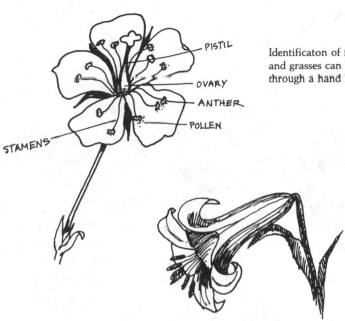

Identificaton of flowers
and grasses can be made
through a hand lens

— Flower Parts. Ask before you pick! Select a large, open blossomed flower for dissection. Look for:

1. pistil — the tube in the center, usually widest at the base;
2. ovary — the swelled base of the pistil;
3. ovules — tiny seedlings inside the ovary;
4. stamens — fuzzy-headed tendrils growing around the pistil;
5. anther — the fuzzy head;
6. pollen — soft powder which brushes off the anthers on touching.

— Live Flowers. Find, clip (with permission, of course) and classify flowers from common grasses, weeds, shrubs, trees, wildflowers and vegetable plants. Keep in a collection box, each stem supported in a small water-filled vial or pill bottle. Keep a desk-top reference book handy in the lab; the keen botanist will also keep a pocket-size field guide on him at all times.

— Pressed Flowers. Look for delicate, small flowers (wild or field varieties are best). Carefully place each one between sheets of newsprint and press by covering the stack with a board and placing a brick or heavy book on top. Leave for a few days, then move the flattened but still moist flowers onto new paper and press again in the same manner, this time leaving them for at least a few weeks.

When completely dry, spray-mount with clear adhesive into a scrap book or onto cardboard, adding a few sprigs of dried grass or weeds for visual interest.

139

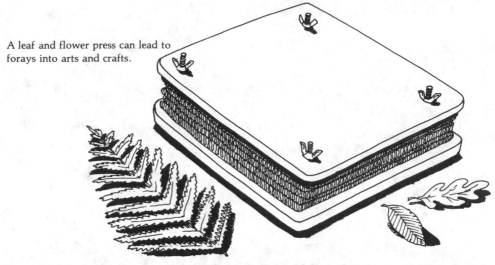

A leaf and flower press can lead to
forays into arts and crafts.

Cover tightly with plastic wrap and tape the back to seal. Help your child date and
classify his work.

If drying becomes a serious hobby, consider making or buying a flower and leaf
press. It's simply a sandwich of thin plywood on the outside with thick cardboard on
the inside, joined at the four corners with bolts and wing nuts. Such a press is
available for about $10 from school suppliers.

— Other Collections. Until you and your child have the system firmly in place,
stick with easily managed collections like rocks and leaves. Progress, with the help
of illustrated texts, to more detailed projects, such as butterflies and beetles.

There are also valuable lessons to be learned about the things around us
without permanently removing them from their natural environment. Here are a
couple of collection games, ideal for picnics and parties.

— Tummy scientist: It may sound juvenile, but this game provides a fun
challenge for all ages. Participants lie on the ground and count (or list) all the things
they can observe through their hand lens without moving an inch.

— Scavenger hunt: In order to make the game really challenging while keeping
the hunters safely limited to the backyard, parents might want to help draft the list.
It should be imaginative and largely non-specific. For example, something that can
make you sneeze, a tiny speck of something, something that makes a noise,
something fuzzy, something square, something perfectly straight, ten of something,
something beautiful, something totally useless, a spore, a weed, a piece of litter, a
chewed leaf (not by humans), a live and unharmed insect, something that makes you
sad, happy and so on.

One important scavenging rule: All things collected must be returned to their
original places. This teaches respect for order while also providing a good memory
challenge.

It's About Time

Few things provide a greater challenge to children than understanding (and marking) the passage of time. They are naturally fascinated by anything that is so clearly out of their control, so relentless and mysterious. Giving a five-year-old a digital watch for her birthday is one sure way of keeping the mystery intact. Helping the child to build a natural clock, on the other hand, is a real gift of time.

Children younger than four have a vague, generally confused notion of time which, while providing some amusing moments for adults, can be totally frustrating to the child. The sooner they get a sense of time's flight, the more accepting they will be of day-to-day routines—like making plans to see a friend tomorrow, or waiting for Mommy to get home from work tonight.

For preschoolers, even the most primitive sun clock can be instructive. A broomstick supported through a hole in an overturned cardboard box will provide a rough shadow-reading of the sun's progress across the sky. They won't be able to read the hours, but this sundial will teach the basic principle of marking time and can be used to indicate the end of playtime or beginning of lunch.

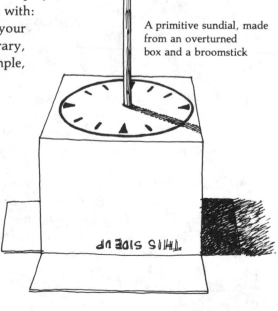

A primitive sundial, made from an overturned box and a broomstick

If you lived on the North Pole, the broomstick-in-a-box clock would give an accurate reading of the hours. Chances are you don't, so you have to tip the sundial so that it faces the sun at the same angle as it would if it were sitting on the pole. Here's a project that older kids can easily help younger ones with:

First, find out what the latitude of your city is. (Ask a reference clerk at the library, or a friendly science teacher.) For example, Los Angeles and San Francisco are both 35 degrees, New York City is 40 degrees, Seattle, Washington, is 45 degrees, Miami is 25 degrees.

Next, subtract your latitude from 90 to get the tilt angle of your sundial. With a protractor (50 cents at a stationery store) mark the angle on a thick piece of cardboard, measure a 4-inch line from the corner of the cardboard through your mark, and cut out the wedge. Then make another wedge just like it.

141

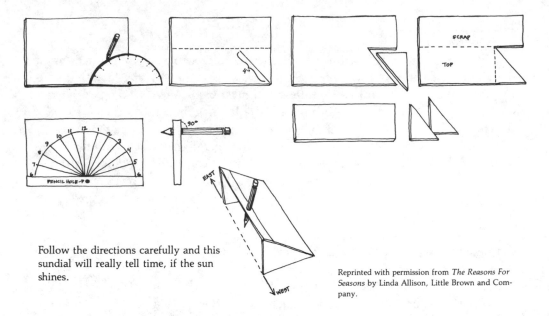

Follow the directions carefully and this sundial will really tell time, if the sun shines.

Reprinted with permission from *The Reasons For Seasons* by Linda Allison, Little Brown and Company.

On a rectangular piece of cardboard about 5 x 11 inches, draw a half-circle and divide it into twelve equal parts. (Use your protractor again for accuracy, measuring the twelve lines 15 degrees apart.) Poke a hole slightly smaller than a pencil at the center where the lines converge, and firmly push the pencil through so that it sits snugly at exactly 90 degrees from the cardboard. Glue the top onto the wedges, and position the sundial along an east-west axis. Now all you need is a little sun.

Silver Linings

Don't despair if the sun fails you. Clouds can provide their own special diversion.

Cloud observation is a serious science—that's how a lot of good meteorologists get their start. Artistic cloud-gazers will want to draw or paint what they see, then classify and (why not?) mount an exhibition of their observations. Watercolors give a lyrical effect. Chalk or pastels on construction paper provide more graphic illustration.

Budding photographers can have a heyday with skyscapes, shooting at different times of the day, over different terrain, even with special-effect filters. Very young children don't need any equipment whatsoever to have a terrific time with clouds, lying back on the grass and simply gazing. Look for animal shapes, construct a cloud castle, let the shapes tell you a story.

The best thing about cloud gazing is you can do it anywhere. When your car pool is inching through rush-hour traffic and nerves are frayed, cast your eyes skyward. Name the types, observe the air currents, forecast tomorrow's weather, start a cloud-picture quiz.

An avid cloud collector must set his sights far beyond his own yard—even beyond his city. Regional cloud patterns differ dramatically. If you live on the coast, you may see lots of stratus but no cirrus clouds; vice versa on the prairie. So why not strike up a correspondence with a long-lost cousin? Swap drawings, magazine clippings or photos through the mail.

ALTO = HIGH
NIMBO OR NIMBUS = ASSOCIATED WITH RAIN

Cloud formations

CUMULUS

CUMULO-NIMBUS

CIRRUS

STRATUS

CIRRO-CUMULUS

NIMBUS

NIMBO-STRATUS

ANIMAL SHAPES

143

...cloud types

Cumulus: White and puffy, stacking like cotton candy up to 12,000 feet in the air; great for picture games; they are generally seen in spring and summer on bright days.

Cirrus: Thin, wispy curls against a blue sky; they streak across the sun as fast as 200 mph, sometimes at heights of 25,000 feet; can occur any time of the year, but because they ride on strong, high winds, they often signal rain or snow on the way.

Stratus: Grayish layers of low-lying clouds, sometimes low enough to be called fog; they are often accompanied by mist or drizzle.

Nimbus: Dark, threatening clouds with no clear shape, usually covering a large area of sky; they signify rain or snow.

Cumulo-nimbus: Also known as thunderheads, these giant, puffy clouds turn steadily darker until they crack open with thunder, lightning and rain; generally seen in summer at the end of a very hot day.

Nimbo-stratus: These are the heavy, dull clouds that pervade an entire sky, obscuring the sun for what seems to be months of the year in coastal regions; often bring rain or snow.

Cirro-cumulus: They ride high, don't pose much of a threat, and sometimes look like puffy fish scales dotting an otherwise blue sky.

Making Feathered Friends

First, decide whether you really want to attract birds to your yard. And if so, which birds? This may call for an item on the next family council agenda. Bird stations and feeders can be a wonderful addition to the backyard, or they can breed pests that devastate your fruit crop and ruin the paint on the hood of your car.

A trip to the library or consultation with your neighborhood bird fancier will help you make a decision. If one of the kids is particularly keen on birds, he should do the legwork and reading. Find out which birds are native to the area, at what time of year they are likely to be hungry, and what they like to eat.

(As a general rule, nonmigrating birds look for food in winter and

The milk-carton bird feeder.

early spring. Many will eat scratch feed, sunflower seeds, corn and millet; some prefer cut fruit, bread crumbs and table scraps.)

You can improvise any kind of feeding tray—a foil pie plate or old baking dish will do—and suspend it from a branch or the eaves of your house, flowerpot fashion. It should be stable enough for the birds to comfortably peck away without having to perform acrobatic feats of balance. Also, be sure the feeder is out of reach to cats or other climbing pets.

Mount it in clear view of a window where you can set up an all-season observatory, stocked with binoculars and note-taking supplies. If you want to go really professional, install a bird blind by fitting a shallow cardboard box into the window frame, open end toward you, with peep holes cut at eye level.

For a deluxe model feeder, cut away one side of a half-gallon milk carton, leaving a 2-inch border around the bottom to support a perch. Use a pencil or 1/4-inch dowel for the perch, and simply poke it through the cardboard border. Hang by a string, or mount the carton on a small wooden platform and nail it to a branch or other high perch. If you're not wild about the way a milk carton looks up the tree, cover it with colored foil or shingle it with popsicle sticks.

In summertime you can add a bath. Any shallow container will do, preferably with sand or gravel sprinkled on the bottom to give the birds a foothold. Keep the water fresh.

The serious ornithologist never lets the birds know he's watching

Catering to Crawlers

Grown-ups spend a lot of energy getting rid of bugs. Kids, on the other hand, can learn a great deal about life's cycles, social instincts and the perfect symmetry of creation by taking a close look at those pesky little varmints. Insects definitely deserve more respect than they get from the average adult, and no one can supply it better than a curious child. Listed below are a few humane ways of getting to know bugs better.

Worm Farm

Get a glass tank (terrarium, fish bowl or large wide-mouthed jar) and topsoil to fill about half the tank. If you have a healthy garden, you've probably helped yourself to a few worms along with the topsoil. Dig around carefully for a few more specimens—use your hands and a small trowel to avoid injuring the worms. It isn't true that you can make two out of one by cutting them in half.

Keep the soil moist and out of direct sunlight. Feed the worms bits of leaves, grass or lettuce, carrot scrapings, cornmeal and cereal grains by mixing them lightly into the top layer of soil. Treat the worms right and you will soon see them tunnelling through the soil, eating their food—they ingest it while tunnelling, then discharge it in the form of castings on the surface of the soil. (Castings are the nutrient-rich gifts worms leave in our gardens.)

Observe your worm farm at night for the most action. Generally they leave their tunnels during nocturnal hunts for food or mates. Watch how they back out tail first, always ready for emergency retreat.

Snail House

You will need a glass container topped with wire screen and a small amount of damp soil, with a few small grass plants and flower seedlings rooted firmly in it.

To find your starter snails, root about the garden in the very early morning. Snails are nocturnal feeders and hide very effectively from the heat of the mid-day sun. Your best clue is the hair-like trail of shimmering slime they leave as they travel between plants.

Keep your specimens in a cool, shady spot, adding bits of food whenever supplies run low. (This will be often. You will be shocked at how much these little fellas can eat.) Experiment with their diet, tossing in bits of leafy green vegetables, bread crumbs, dead insects, or crumbled hamburger.

Watch for sudden increases in population. Like worms, every snail is both male and female—each one capable of having babies. Keep the population down by constantly returning a few specimens to the garden.

Don't be disheartened if some of the snails depart for the big pearly shell in the sky. Chances are they would have died just as soon in your garden. Remove the dead ones, and if your child is so inclined, he might want to wash the shells out thoroughly with soapy water, dry and mount them as a display of nature's remarkable coloration and camouflage patterns. They can even be threaded (you will need a very sharp needle, and steady aim) for shell jewelry.

Insect Dorm

Use a glass or clear plastic container with a lid, air holes punched in, with bits of growing grass and sod, twigs, leaves and small stones.

Look for different types of larvae—caterpillars, tomato worms, maggots (fly larvae) or whatever happens to be hatching in your neighborhood. Keep types of larvae in separate jars, label the date of capture and suspected or confirmed type. Try to duplicate the food each type was eating when captured, adding fresh bits daily. Notice how much these creatures can eat, and how quickly they grow.

When they've eaten so much that they can barely budge, the larva stage is over and the pupa stage about to begin. They will enclose themselves in a case (the most fascinating to watch is the caterpillar spinning its silken cocoon) and in many cases stay cozy and warm that way all winter. Find a secure outdoor location for your little dorms, but don't forget about them. The transition to adult insects in spring is the most spectacular to watch (hand lens ready!), and liberation from the dorm into the fresh spring air is the most rewarding experience of all.

Ant Town

You'll need a glass mason jar, at least one-quart size, with a screw-on sealer lid, but instead of the sealer, insert a circle of fine wire screen over the jar top.

Before scooping an unsuspecting colony of ants into the jar, the child should get down on the ground with his hand lens and study the way these highly social creatures operate in their natural environment. Sprinkle a few grains of sugar onto

an anthill; then try grass seed. Watch how various other natural foods disappear into the mound. Make note of their favorite meals. Watch them come and go, moving along their trails, avoiding collision with ants going the opposite way.

Carefully scoop enough of the mound into the jar to fill it three-quarters full. Using a leaf or piece of paper, pick up stray ants from the same mound and lightly tap them into the jar. Sprinkle a few drops of water onto the top of the soil, add a sprinkling of sugar, grass seed and a sampling of other favored foods. Also place a 1-inch-square piece of wet sponge on the soil.

Wrap the jar in dark cloth or paper, and seal with the wire screen. Unwrap only for observation, and to feed every few days. If the intricate tunnelling, transporting and "personal hygiene" of the ants isn't enough to keep children transfixed, try introducing a few new (different sized, different colored) ants to the town to see how they fare.

CHAPTER 10

Artsplay

The kids have spent the whole morning burning off steam outdoors. Time for them to calm down, to quietly play with a favorite toy, maybe stretch out in the hammock with a book or settle down at the picnic table with pastels and paper.

This may also be the time for you to make your move—to cozy up and get involved with your kids in a quiet-time activity. There's still time before the dinner hour. Take advantage of it.

It suddenly struck me during my daughter's fifth year that it was time to check the balance in our relationship. Her dad and I had spent a good deal of time and energy up to that point gently prying her away from the tight physical dependence of infancy. And we were starting to see results: She could now initiate her own projects, she preferred the company of peers to adults, and was capable of solving her own problems without making undue demands on her parents or resorting to temper tantrums. Then suddenly it dawned on us—if this keeps up, she'll be happily packing her bags and moving out by age six.

Fortunately, it is precisely at this preschool age that most children develop the ability to devote concentrated time to a single activity. From the parent's viewpoint, spending time with their children can change radically, from mental drain to companionship and mutual stimulation. But parents must learn to take advantage of their child's budding maturity. Too often we remain in the "go-out-and-play" mode, missing precious opportunities to sit down and work or play together.

It is important to establish a stimulating relationship in these preschool years, because by the time most children reach school age they will naturally develop a strong preference for their peers. And so they should, but not at the expense of family values and relationships. If the growing child savors the special moments spent at home with parents and siblings, he will feel more secure about venturing out with peers, and more competent when faced with new challenges.

The Backyard Artist

Arts and crafts fill different functions for different ages. Preschoolers tend to take them on as a manual challenge more than a creative experience. They can get wildly excited about mastering the use of scissors. Learning to hold a felt pen properly can make their whole day. They will be consumed by any simple project that stretches their fine motor abilities beyond yesterday's horizons.

Older children (five to fourteen) are more oriented toward the results of their creativity, though they will still enjoy the process of creating if it's made interesting to them. In fact, these are the crucial years in creative development. Without opportunities and encouragement, many children will lose their sense of spontaneous expression. This will inhibit not only artistic ability but also creative problem solving in later life.

Private or school art classes fill a certain void for many children, but they cannot replace creative experimentation at home. Unfortunately, parents may think

they can get themselves "off the hook" by signing their kids up for lessons. What they may not realize is they're also signing themselves out of a priceless opportunity to get to know their kids better.

There is no better place for creative experimentation than at home, under the benevolent supervision of a parent or friend. This is especially true with school-age children who are often too sensitive to criticism and generally too guarded about their group status to let their creative flood gates open at school.

A back porch or deck makes an ideal open-air arts and crafts studio, not only because it saves messing up the house, but because the natural surroundings can be inspirational to fledgling artists. New ideas will spring forth daily, as natural treasures are observed and collected from both your yard and neighborhood.

...stocking the art cupboard

Looking through an art supply catalog can also be inspirational, whether you intend to buy the stuff or not. I sat down one afternoon with the Galt catalog and came up with projects to fill up an entire Christmas break.

If my daughters held the purse strings, we would now be the proud owners of two different sized easels, an art-drying frame, a pound of polystyrene balls for collage and model making, a generous sampling of the thirty-nine different paint brushes, a dozen types of felt pens, a brilliant palette of paints in powder, liquid and watercolor form, plus child-safe glue for spraying, spreading, mixing with paint, mounting on paper, and working with fabric or wood—all of it clear drying and easily washed off fingers and clothes.

Don't go out and buy all of this for your kids—at least not all at once. But whatever you do decide on, look for family-sized quantities (especially of basic supplies like paint, glue and paper). You'll find the best prices at teacher supply shops, if you can get in. By all means, take your kids with you, but first draft a shopping list and try to stick to it. (Don't leave your own preferences off the list. After all, the idea is for you to get involved along with the kids.)

A Sample Shopping List

— Powdered paint in a range of colors (premixed liquid color is handy, but more expensive) and plastic cups for mixing the paint—look for the type with snap-on, spill-resistant lids and rubber stoppers to minimize evaporation.

— Chunky brushes for children younger than three. A range of fine, medium and chunky brushes for older children (you should be able to get a mixed set of brushes for less than a dollar). Buy from a reputable manufacturer—you will pay pennies more for a brush that will last months longer.

— Watercolor set, with a similar range of brush sizes.

— A few nylon detailing brushes for the budding Rembrandt. Quality fine-pointed brushes cost more than the chunkies (up to two dollars each), but how else are you going to capture the markings on a butterfly's wing?

— Chubby crayons for tiny fingers; a selection of regular crayons, oil or water-based pastels, pencil crayons and felts for older kids. There is such a staggering selection on the market these days (water-based pastels that can be wet-brushed for effect; metallic markers for decoration; paint sticks for fabric art) that you might want to let your kids make some choices. Keep some of the really fancy markers in mind for gifts.

— Powdered all-purpose adhesive, safe for children and easily washed out of clothes. This is the cheapest way to buy glue, and the most practical because you can mix it to different consistencies (or add it to paint) depending on the project. Mixed thick for young children, it can be dished out in small quantities and applied with popsicle sticks. Older kids will prefer using refillable dispensers with proper spreaders for finer work. Gluesticks are extremely handy, but they don't last long.

— Modelling materials. Although many people make their own varieties (recipes on page 156), you can buy a wide range of materials in beautiful rainbow colors. Playdough is a mainstay for toddlers because it's so pliable; stiffer modelling clay and papier-mache mixtures offer more of a challenge to school-age kids.

— Rubber mats, boards, linoleum pieces or oilcloth on which to do modelling.

— A variety of paper (you can't get enough): newsprint; computer sheets; white or brown wrapping paper in rolls, or any other ready supply of cheap paper for rough work; plain white or manila paper for drawing; construction, kraft or poster paper for painting and making collages; and butcher paper for finger painting.

— Small scissors. Be sure to choose appropriate left- or right-handed models, with blunt ends for children younger than five.

— Fastening materials: stapler, clips, tacks and tape. In a windy yard, you won't even be able to start a paper project without fastening the sheets to a board or easel.

— A wide assortment of fuzzy, shiny, pliable, stiff, round, square and ridiculous materials to work with. Generally, kids can scrounge up many of these things from the house, yard and neighborhood. But occasionally you may want to buy something really special to get the creative juices flowing. Some of our family favorites are: specialty colored papers and stickers; pipe cleaners; polystyrene or styrofoam shapes; popsicle sticks, tongue depressors and other wooden pieces; sparkles, beads and fake gems; dyed feathers; copper wire; rafia; pliable construction straws; stamping kits; cartons and containers of all kinds; and an assortment of covered containers (shoe boxes, cookie tins and the like) to organize these bits and pieces.

...setting up the studio

No matter what age your children are, you will find the easel to be one of the most versatile and enduring pieces of play equipment you can buy. Or why not build one, if you are even a bit handy? (Older children can help.) Here is a simple design:

Double easel

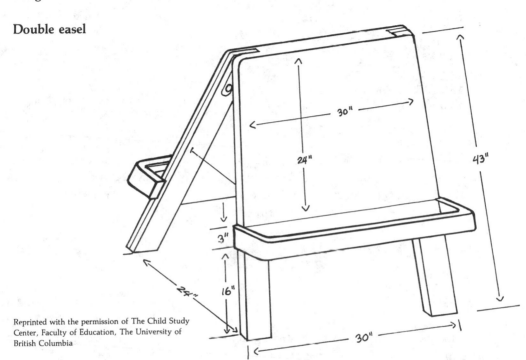

Reprinted with the permission of The Child Study Center, Faculty of Education, The University of British Columbia

Materials

 2 pieces 1/4-inch plywood, cut 30 x 24 inches for painting surface panels
 172 inches of 1-inch x 2-1/2-inch fir or alder, cut to 4 lengths for uprights
 78 inches of 3/8-inch x 3-inch softwood, cut to two 30-inch and four 4-1/2-inch
   lengths to frame the paint bottle racks
 30 inches of 1/2-inch x 4-inch softwood, for base of racks
 two 4-inch strap hinges
 2 large hooks and eyes for leg braces (if large enough hooks can't be found, use
   card table braces)

Construction

Cut and carefully sand all pieces, planing edges and rounding corners. Using standard box nails (countersink heads), frame the paint bottle racks and attach to legs. Finish with at least two coats of varnish or outdoor paint. Connect the painting panels at the top with strap hinges, and brace the legs. If the easel will also be used indoors, glue rubber stripping to the bottom of the uprights to save wear on your floors.

...homemade gooeys

Playdough

> 2 cups flour
> 1 cup salt
> 2 tsp. creme of tartar
> 3 tbsp. salad oil
> 2 cups water
> food coloring

Mix dry ingredients in a medium-size soup pot. Add oil. Stir desired color into water and mix into the pot. Cook on medium heat, stirring constantly, until all moisture is gone and dough has a rubbery texture. Remove from heat, allow to cool for a few minutes and knead thoroughly.

Paper Paste

> 2 cups flour
> 1/2 cup sugar
> 6 cups water

Mix and cook over low heat, stirring, until mixture is almost transparent. Store paste in a large jar in the refrigerator, and dish out when required in small containers. Powdered paint or food coloring can be added for interest.

Finger paint

> 1/2 cup instant cold-water starch
> 1 cup pure soap flakes
> 2/3 cup water
> powdered paint

Beat well, until mixture forms a smooth, thick paste. Divide into smaller portions and add a different color to each. These can be covered and stored on the shelf for long periods, but more water must be added to keep the consistency. Young children will enjoy using this gooey paint with their brushes as well. Its added density makes for richer colors and much less dripping than ordinary liquid paint.

Glue mixed with food coloring makes liquid stained glass.

Liquid stained glass

    powdered or liquid white paste
    food coloring
    copper wire or pipe cleaners

If you are using powdered glue, mix with water to make a runny paste —enough to fill a small bowl. Add the food coloring of your choice. Shape the wire into small flowers, stars, hearts or any other looped form, and dip into the paste. Mount these on styrofoam or hang in windows.

Sawdust clay

    8 cups sawdust
    4 cups wallpaper paste
    water

In a large bowl, pour enough water into the paste to make it creamy. Add sawdust to desired consistency. Work until smooth, on clay table or other protected surface. This modelling mixture is great for rough sculptures, such as fort-building, landscapes and the like. Add an interesting finish with paint or spray lacquer.

157

Cornstarch clay

> 1 cup cornstarch
> 4 cups salt
> 4 cups boiling water

Boil to soft-ball stage, stirring constantly. Remove from heat, cool and knead until smooth. Store in plastic.

Drawing Them Out

Making art a social as well as creative experience can enhance relationships among parents and children, siblings and friends. All you've got to do is make art fun. (And believe me, when children are involved it's much harder to make art tedious.) Given a wide choice of materials and a little imagination, you can hardly miss. Try these ideas, adapting in your own way to the age group involved.

Painting Big

This one uses up a lot of paint, paper and bath water. (You might want to save it for special times when you all feel energetic and expansive.) Use large sheets of mural paper, or rolls of plain wrapping paper. Provide gooey finger-type paint, and encourage any and all experimentation with hands, feet, brushes, sponges, rope for dipping, potato cuttings for printing.

Add to the sensual experience by turning on some favorite music. Finger and hand painting should be done standing up, with paper lying flat on a table or mounted on a board. Sitting inhibits the body movements and rhythms that will come through the music onto the paper. The idea is to encourage interplay between what goes in the ear and what comes out the fingers. Discuss the experience over a quiet cup of milk afterwards.

Children should be allowed to mix their own paint, especially outdoors where you can afford to be fairly casual about spills. The best part of experimentation with colors and textures goes on at the mixing stage, especially among the very young who are only beginning to develop their visual and tactile senses. By sparking their interest at the outset, concentration will be increased for the entire activity. And naturally, they will reap more pleasure in the results.

Painted shells and marbles
make a miniature parade

MARBLE

Painting tiny

This project is especially suited to groups with a wide range of ages. The youngest members will naturally concentrate on the scavenging aspect, while the older ones can challenge themselves on finely detailed painting.

Everyone starts by scavenging. Kids will need small stones, nut shells, pieces of bark — anything bigger than a beetle but smaller than a plum. (Younger children should be encouraged to find slightly larger objects.) Using fine brushes and thick paint (acrylic works best) children unleash their imaginations on these inanimate objects to bring them to life as rock animals, porcu-pinecones, or whatever comes to mind. For a nifty nut idea, paint a half walnut shell to resemble a small animal or car, fit a marble inside and let it roll.

Entire tiny zoos, farms, cities or airports can be created over time. Encourage the kids to start collections in suitable boxes or trays, and to add to them whenever they find more paintable objects. Keep these materials neatly tucked away but ever accessible, to encourage self-initiation.

Evocative drawing

There are dozens of variations to this activity, some suited to quiet doodling, others perfect for party games. Once your kids get a taste for it, they'll be inventing their own.

The most basic form is the circle story. Seat everyone around a table, and have them all draw something on a set theme—perhaps animals, children playing, people working, or cars and trucks. When everyone is finished, they pass their drawings to the people on their right who (in turn) make up stories about what they see. These should be simple thirty-second tales for young children, more elaborate yarns for school-age children—possibly using a continuing narrative from one storyteller to the next. The game is most fluid when the players are roughly the same age.

As a child, my favorite variation was "drawing in the dark" in which my two sisters and I crowded into a pitch-black closet, clutching drawing pads and pencils, and tried to sketch something meaningful. When we were finished we'd tumble out into the light, pass our drawings around and see if the next person could correctly guess what we had drawn. The game used to go on for hours, until my little sister eventually got spooked by mysterious ghost sounds coming from the depths of the closet. On rainy or cold days, try this one in the basement.

Some evocative variations

Scribble art: A piece of paper or index card gets passed around, each person adding a scribble to produce an end product worth guessing at.

Cumulative drawing: A figure or any representative drawing is begun by one child and finished in stages as it is passed along. (The children may wish to combine this exercise with a matching "cumulative story.")

Blot art: A figure or entire story may be suggested by the shape of a blotted blob of paint. Drop thick paint on porous paper (or dip a string into paint and lay it on the paper in an interesting pattern), then fold the paper in half to blot it.

Prints and Rubbings

A messy prospect indoors, printmaking is an ideal back porch activity. Again, the possibilities are endless. Start with a tray of medium-thick paint, a variety of brush shapes and other applicators (rubber spatulas and sponges work well) and the most basic printing forms around — fingers, hands and feet. Save hot wax printing for the experts.

You can move on to potato printing (an adult should wield the knife to carve stamping forms into potato halves), or experiment with found objects from your yard. Finely coat leaves or flower petals with paint and press gently between two sheets of tissue paper. Or try different effects with feathers.

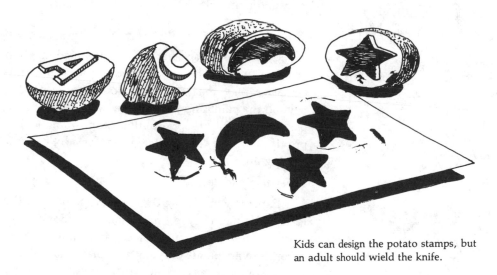

Kids can design the potato stamps, but an adult should wield the knife.

Rubbings give another perspective on the texture of found objects. Comb the house for bits of scrap carpet, paper doilies, window screen or coins; look outdoors for interesting leaves, bark and feathers. Put a collection of these items between two sheets of fine paper, and rub gently over the top with chalk or crayon.

Junk sculpture and collages

Here's another way to recycle useless bits of household and backyard litter. The "beautiful junk collage" is especially suited to young children because it is basically a paper and glue affair. Combine as many media as your space (and tolerance for mess) allows. Paint, crumpled tissue paper, torn bits of colored construction paper, sparkles and other fineries can be combined with rough patches of sand, twigs, dinky-toy wheels, dried weeds and so on.

Let the kids' imaginations loose. Don't censure ideas (unless they pose a safety risk). Children will discover certain crucial principles for themselves: like the point at which gravity will overpower glue, and the consequences of spraying the entire collage with a garden hose.

This activity can be repeated frequently, sustaining interest by changing themes and materials. Try an architectural theme one day, providing small pieces of wood, popsicle sticks, shavings and multi-colored squares of paper. Or a forest theme can be explored with bits of greenery for flora and tufts of fur and feathers for fauna.

As their dexterity develops, children will enjoy the challenge of building table-top sculptures with a base of clay, wood or wire, adding found materials to provide the detailing.

Puppets, masks and dolls

Creativity doesn't have to end upon completion of the artwork. The art can become a prop in imaginative play that continues hours or even days beyond the paint and paper stage. Masks, for example, offer magical opportunities for dramatic improvisations—or, in kids' language, for a lot of great horsing around.

Paper bag people

Paper bag masks are the easiest to make, but the least enduring. They're fine for an afternoon's play: Just cut holes for eyes, nose and mouth, then decorate with paint, crayons and pieces of colored wool. If you have an abundance of paper grocery bags, create a wardrobe in the same vein. Cut holes for head and arms and you have an instant tunic. Cut a larger waist hole, cinch the opening with a belt and you've got a skirt. (Pants are trickier.)

Why stop at a paper bag mask? Make a whole costume.

Use old bed linens for more permanent masks. Cut them into 12- x 20-inch pieces, sew them together on three sides to form small sacks, and turn inside out to obscure the seams. Cut holes for the face and embellish with felt shapes, ribbon, wool, feathers and colored markers. This is a good learn-to-sew project for children older than four. Younger tots can use double-sided tape to attach decorative pieces.

Hats

A simpler project, ideal for parties, is hat making. Start with a 12-inch circle of light cardboard or heavy construction paper. Make one radial cut, and staple into a broad cone shape. Attach elastic or ribbon by piercing the cone in two places near the rim.

Individualize the hats by adding a fringe of hair (attach paper strips or coils with glue or double-sided tape); bows, flowers and feathers add a decorative touch. For a party idea, let each child write her name in glue and apply sparkles. For Halloween, of course, make black hats, add a rim and other witchy touches.

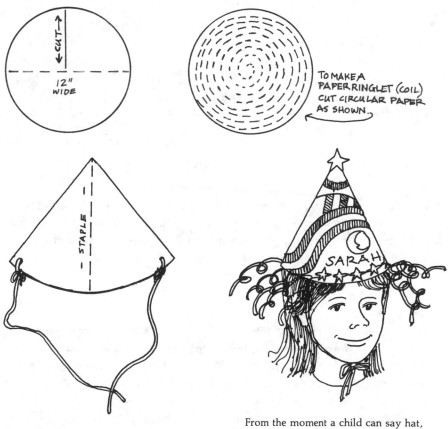

From the moment a child can say hat, he wants to make one.

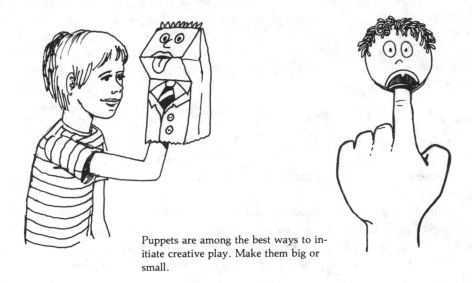

Puppets are among the best ways to initiate creative play. Make them big or small.

Paper bag puppets

Puppets are great for promoting imaginative play because children are much less guarded about the things they'll let their fingers or fists say than what might normally come out of their mouths. Slip an old sock over the fist, attach a button or pom-pom for nose, draw in the eyes and mouth and you have an adorable hand puppet. Small paper bags make a handy disposable version, and under supervision even small children can cut a two-inch slit along one folded edge for the mouth.

Finger puppets

Or make tiny finger puppets by gluing two paper circles (two inches in diameter) together, leaving a half-inch hole in the bottom. Get out your magnifying glass for the finishing touches on these tiny puppets. Make several at a time, encouraging finger games and plays afterward. Each finger can wear a different emotion for a play about feelings. Or create a family of finger puppets and watch the kids act out their adaptations of real family life.

Apple puppets

For a challenge, older kids can carve apple-head puppets. With a small paring knife, peel and hollow out a large apple (you might want to do this part); let the kids carve into it slowly, chipping away small bits of pulp until a face emerges; soak it in salt water for a half-hour, then put the apple head in a warm dry place. The result will be a crazy, wrinkled face—perfect for madcap comedy or Greek tragedy. Combine with a sock body or small sack shape made of any scrap fabric. Cut holes for finger-arms to pop out. Decorate with the usual beautiful junk.

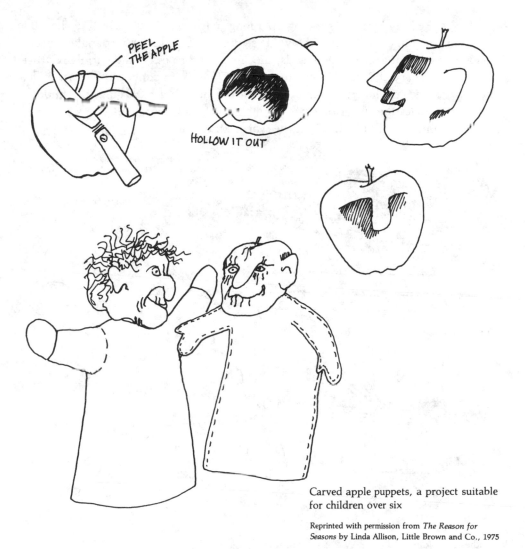

PEEL THE APPLE

HOLLOW IT OUT

Carved apple puppets, a project suitable for children over six

Reprinted with permission from *The Reason for Seasons* by Linda Allison, Little Brown and Co., 1975

Corn husk dolls

It's amazing what rich resources dwell in an average family's garbage can. Corn husks, for example. Here's a centuries-old design for corn husk dolls, originating among the Indian tribes of the Eastern Seaboard. Kids age eight and older can do most of the work themselves; younger ones may require help.

All you need is a pile of husks and some string. Start with the doll's hair: Tie a bundle of silks tightly in the middle. (All knots must be extremely tight to hold the doll together.) Cut the silks, leaving at least two inches of hairs on each side of the knot. Strip the husks and shrink them by leaving them to dry in a warm place for six hours. Soak in hot water if they become stiff.

Make the head by tightly rolling up a long, narrow strip of husk. Put the silks on top of the roll, cover both with a wide strip and tie underneath to make a neck. Roll a long strip for arms; tie both ends, slide it under the neck and tie firmly. Gather some husks around the waist and tie for a skirt. Divide into pants and tie for a male. Use a wide rectangular piece for a shirt, cutting it halfway through the middle, lengthwise. Place the uncut half behind the doll, fold the two cut strips over the shoulders and cross in front. Tie at the waist. Draw faces.

Reprinted with permission from *The Reason for Seasons* by Linda Allison, Little Brown and Co., 1975

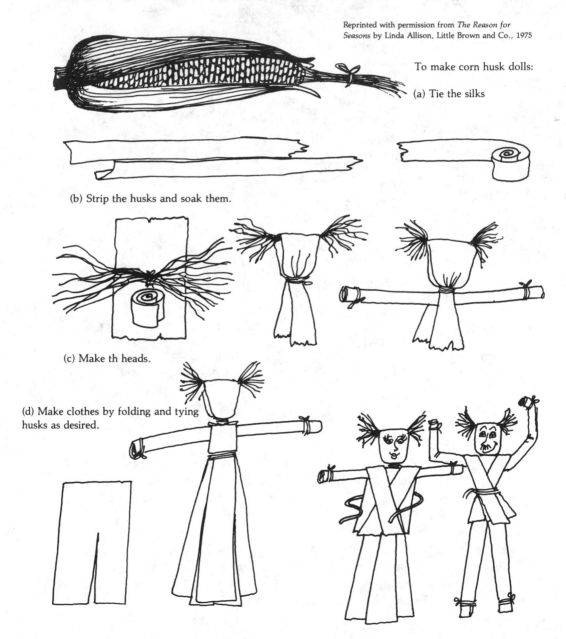

To make corn husk dolls:

(a) Tie the silks

(b) Strip the husks and soak them.

(c) Make th heads.

(d) Make clothes by folding and tying husks as desired.

Drama on the Deck

The best way to adapt dramatic play to your backyard is to simply bring out the prop and costume box. If you don't have one, now's the time to start a collection. Fill any box or bin with odds and ends from around the house—old clothes, scrap fabric, old Halloween costumes, a spare umbrella, broken camera or obsolete telephone—any old thing will do.

You'll probably find that over time, prop collection becomes a family hobby. You will find yourselves returning from vacation with suitcases stuffed full of gifts like Hawaiian grass skirts and coconut hats for the costume box rather than the standard T-shirts and bikinis. Soon word will get out to Grandma who'll drop by with a serpent-headed cane she found in a curiosity shop, or Uncle Willard who might donate an original Davy Crockett hat.

Of course the kids are bound to get into the action too. Soon nothing in the house will escape their scrutiny. (Watch out for over enthusiastic scavengers. You wouldn't want to see your fine porcelain drop-kicked into the drama cupboard.)

Once you have a healthy collection, dramatic play will naturally proceed at its own pace and in its own fashion—depending on the age and whims of your children. You may want to get involved at times, for your own entertainment. Occasionally you'll be required to participate as an audience. As in all things relating to the people we love, we get back at least as much as we put in.

...dress-up drama for tots

Young kids are natural actors, but you may want to help preschoolers structure their drama, to get them off and running. Help them gather the costumes and set the stage for improvisations on familiar themes.

Playing house. They can draw burners on an overturned box for a stove; use a water table or any plastic tub for a sink; furniture can be improvised using hollow blocks or cardboard crates. Let the kids raid the house for unbreakables—plastic dishes and utensils, old pots and pans, spare towels and linens. You can be certain someone will play the baby, loudly. Someone might get hurt, someone else slighted. If you play it right, they are likely to solve their own little familial problems very admirably.

Grocery store. This is another favorite among preschoolers. I suppose the reason they love it so much is that they so often find themselves powerless in the real situation—confined to a seat in the shopping cart, unable to affect the choice of groceries or the speed of the cart. All they need to create their own shopping drama is a counter, carts and lots of stuff to buy. Add a toy cash register or shoe box, poker chips or buttons for cash, paper and pencils for pricing, dress-up items for the shopper (hat, coat, purse or wallet) and the shopkeeper (apron, name tag, bow tie), and they're in business.

Let them take certain foodstuffs from the kitchen, like sealed cans, a bag of oranges or a box of dried food. You can help to make this an instructive experience by encouraging shopkeepers to categorize items according to type, size, weight, storage temperature and freshness.

Restaurant, fix-it shop, gas station, airport. Before long you won't have to suggest themes to your kids. They'll come up with their own steady supply.

...a little more challenge

Children older than four are capable of greater feats of imagination with less reliance on material props. (But don't burn the dress-up box. They will continue to find pleasure and inspiration there for years to come.) For a change, however, you might encourage them to test their creative powers through pantomime in its many forms.

Charades: The most popular pantomime game, it's ideal for children's parties because it can be played on any level to match ability. Start simply with action quizzes: The child does something specific to a place, and the other kids have to guess where he is. Similarly, they can guess what he's eating, what he's riding in, what clothes he's wearing or what job he's doing.

Animal Crackers: Guess what the main prop for this game is? (If you don't like sugary snacks, look for whole-grain, honey-sweetened animal crackers at your supermarket. Or better yet, make your own with animal-shaped cookie cutters.) The idea here is "you are what you eat." Each child picks a cracker out of the box or hat, keeping it hidden from the rest of the group. To earn the right to eat the cracker, she must act it out in front of the group and they must guess what animal she is.

Improvisational theater: Odd items (field glasses, a garden hoe, bath sponge, dictionary) are assembled in a deep box or bin, out of plain view. Sketches performed by individual actors or small groups are improvised around one or more items picked from the box. In a large gathering of children, a panel of peers may be chosen to judge each improvisation and award points or prizes.

Shadow play: Depending on the lay of your yard, this activity will be limited to certain hours of sunny days—probably late on summer afternoons. String up a light-colored sheet (you can pin it to the ground from a clothesline) and group the actors on the west side of it, the audience on the east. Depending on the angle of sunlight, you will get different effects. The medium is ripe for experimentation—from the sublime to the ridiculous. Add props, such as large balls, blocks and heavy rope. Use music for extra effect. Or you can scale the whole thing down to pillowslip-size for hand shadow theater.

Animatronics: Every neighborhood has a different version of this drama game. Basically, it's about setting inanimate objects into motion. The objects can be statues, wind-up toys or wooden soldiers. The children can take turns acting as the

objects and the animator—by winding up or pushing a button, the objects come to life. An entire drama can unfold thereafter—like *The Nutcracker Suite*.

...bang, bang, toot, toot!

Children absolutely must make noise, sometimes. It is fair to control the level inside the house, but cruel to keep the stopper in all day long. A well-proven strategy (in our home, anyway) is to avoid berating children for making too much noise. If you get angry, they get angry and the noise level has only one way to go. In firm, civil language, suggest that loud or irritating noises would sound just fine outdoors. Keep the back door open.

Music can be part of any creative experience, or an end in itself. And what better place to drum up interest than outdoors. Once outside, kids can do all kinds of creative venting. Simple rhythm instruments can be made with odds and ends. Outfit an entire marching band with coffee-can drums, broomstick pieces, pot-lids and shakers made from plastic containers and dried peas.

Older kids will be intrigued with the possibility of chimes. Cut a broomstick or dowel to different lengths, drill a hole through the end of each and string them up in a row. Use a 1-inch dowel or a rhythm stick to strike them. (Add an extra dimension to the project by decorating the wooden chimes with acrylic paint.) Water chimes can be made by filling a row of glass jars to different depths and striking with a fine stick or metal pipe.

For a group jam session, let the kids raid the house and garage for any and all music-making objects. Assemble real, toy and makeshift instruments on the porch, and strike up the band. A portable tape recorder can be invaluable at times like these, to record the symphony or to play some favorite songs for the kids to jam with.

Appendix I

A Directory of English-Language Organizations

American Adventure Play Association
Fort Mason Center, San Francisco, California 94123, U.S.

Association for Childhood Education International
3615 Wisconsin Avenue North West, Washington, D.C. 20016, U.S.

British Standard Institute
(Recreation Division) 2 Park Street, London W1A 2BS, England

Canada Mortgage and Housing Corporation
(Children's Environments Advisory Service) 682 Montreal Road, Ottawa, Ontario K1A 0P7, Canada

Canada Safety Council
1765 St. Laurent Boulevard, Ottawa, Ontario K1G 3V4, Canada

Canadian Association for Health, Physical Education and Recreation
333 River Road, Vanier City, Ontario K1L 8B9, Canada

Canadian Association of Toy Libraries
Suite 1207, 50 Quebec Avenue, Toronto, Ontario M6P 4B4, Canada

Canadian Council on Children and Youth
323 Chapel Street, Ottawa, Ontario K1N 7Z2, Canada

Canadian Parks and Recreation Association
333 River Road, Vanier City, Ontario K1L 8B9, Canada

Canadian Standards Association
178 Rexdale Boulevard, Rexdale, Ontario M9W 1R3, Canada

Canadian Toy Testing Council
P.O. Box 6014, Station J, Ottawa, Ontario K2A 1T1, Canada

Center for Architecture and Urban Planning
(Children's Environments Project) University of Wisconsin, P.O. Box 413, Milwaukee, Wisconsin 53201, U.S.

Center for Human Environments
(Environmental Psychology Program) Graduate Center of the City University of New York, 33 West 42nd Street, New York, N.Y. 10036, U.S.

Children's Play Resource Center
3644 Slocan Street, Vancouver, British Columbia V5M 3E8, Canada

Consumer Product Safety Commission
Office of the Secretary, 5401 Westbard Avenue, Bethesda, Maryland 20207, U.S.

Consumers' Association of Canada
801 - 257 Laurier Avenue West, Ottawa, Ontario K1N 6P8, Canada

Department of Consumer and Corporate Affairs
(Recreational and Children's Products) 16th floor, Place du Portage, 68 Victoria Street, Hull, Quebec K1A 0C9, Canada

Educational Design and Consultants
3259 North Shore Road, Bellingham, Washington 98225, U.S.

Handicapped Adventure Playground Association
Fulham Palace, Bishops Avenue, London SW6 6EA, England

International Association for the Child's Right to Play: (formerly the International Playground Association)

—**England:** 12 Cherry Tree Drive, Sheffield, S11 9AE

—**United States:** c/o Mr. Robin Moore, School of Design, North Carolina State University, P.O. Box 7701, Raleigh, North Carolina 27695

—**Canada:** c/o Ms Jane Knight, 1391 Halifax Place, Burlington, Ontario L7S 1J7

—**Scotland:** c/o Ms Nancy L.G. Ovens, 3 Denham Green Avenue, Edinburgh EH5 3NY

—**Australia:** c/o Ms Nan Lukey, 225 Point Lonsdale Road, Point Lonsdale, Victoria 3225

—**New Zealand:** c/o Ms Elizabeth Hanan, 159 Highgate, Dunedin

National Association for the Education of Young Children
1834 Connecticut Avenue North West, Washington, D.C. 20009, U.S.

National Day Care Information Center
(Social Service Programs Branch) Health and Welfare Canada, Tunney's Pasture, Ottawa, Ontario K1A 1B5, Canada

National Playing Fields Association
25 Ovington Square, London SW3 1LQ, England

Play and Parenting Connections
301 Montrose Avenue, Toronto, Ontario M6G 3G9, Canada

Play School Association
111 East 59th Street, 13th floor, New York, N.Y. 10022, U.S.

Playground Clearing House Inc.
26 Buckwalter Road, Phoenixville, Pennsylvania 19460, U.S.

Playgrounds and Recreation Association of Victoria
346 Albert, Brunswick, Melbourne 3056, Australia

Standards Association of New Zealand
6th floor, Wellington Trade Center, 181 - 187 Victoria Street, Wellington 1, N.Z.

Toy Libraries Association
Seabrook House, Wyllyotts Manor, Darkes Lane, Potters Bar, Hertfordshire EN6 2HL, England

World Leisure and Recreation Association
345 East 46th Street, New York, N.Y. 10017, U.S.

World Organization for Early Childhood Education
81 Irving Place, New York, N.Y. 10003, U.S.

Appendix II
Poisonous and Hazardous Plants

Listed below are common landscape plants which may be poisonous to children. In general, they should not be planted in areas where children will be playing for extended periods. Some are safer than others on a limited contact basis. Check with your local poison control center for details before planting. Also be sure to check toxicity of native or exotic plants not included on this list.

Trees

Common Name	Proper Name
Aralia/Japanese angelica	Aralia elata
Beech - all species, particularly the European	Fagus spp. (particularly the sylvatica)
Cherry	Prunus (all species)
Black locust	Robinia pseudo-acacia
Golden chain	Laburnum anagyroides
Horse chestnut	Aesculus spp.
Kentucky coffee tree	Gymnocladus dioica
Oak	Quercus spp.
Red mulberry	Morus rubra
Sumac (Staghorn)	Rhus typhina
Yew - all species	Taxus spp.

Shrubs

Azalea	Rhododendron spp.
Box/Boxwood	Buxus sempervirens
Buckeye	Aesculus spp.
Buckthorn	Rhamnus spp.
Burning bush/Spindle tree	Euonymus spp.
Daphne	Daphne spp.

173

Common Name	Proper Name
Elderberry	Sambucus
Holly	Ilex spp.
Hydrangea	Hydrangea spp.
Jetbead/Jetberry bush	Rhodotypos tetrapetala Makino
Lantana	Lantana camara
Laurel/Cherry laurel	Prunus laurocerasus var.
Leucothoe	Leucothoe
Mountain laurel	Kalmia latifolia
Oleander	Nerium oleander
Pieris/Lilly-of-the-valley	Pieris japonica
Privet	Ligustrum vulgare
Rhododendron	Rhododendron spp.
Snowberry/Waxberry	Symphoricarpos spp.
Strawberry bush	Euonymus spp.
Yew	Taxus spp.

Vines

Clematis	Clematis spp.
English ivy	Hedera helix
Periwinkle	Vinca minor
Virginia creeper	Parthenocissus quinquefolia
Wisteria	Wisteria sinensis

Herbaceous Plants, Annuals and Perennials

Anemone	Anemone spp.
Autumn crocus	Colchicum autumnale
Bleeding heart	Dicentra spp.
Bluebell/scilla	Scilla nonscripta peruviana
Buttercup	Ranunculus spp.
Castor bean	Ricinus communis
Coneflower	Rudbeckia hortensis Bailey
Delphinium	Delphinium spp.
Foxglove	Digitalis purpurea

Common Name	Proper Name	
Hyacinth	Hyacinthus orientalis	*Appendices*
Lily-of-the-valley	Convallaria majalis	
Lobelia	Lobelia spp.	
Lupine	Lupinus spp.	
Monkshood	Aconitum nepellus	
Narcissus/jonquil/daffodil	Narcissus spp.	
Star of Bethlehem	Ornithogalum umbellatum	
Tansy	Tanacetum vulgare	

Food Plant Parts

Rhubarb — leaves

Cherry trees — twigs and leaves

Avocado — leaves

Tomato — leaves and stem

Potato — sprouts

Reprinted with permission from The Playground Network, Vancouver, Canada

Appendix III

Selected Body Dimensions of Toddlers and Preschoolers

The following tables will assist in designing play equipment that affords optimum enjoyment and safety for the very young child. As well, playthings scaled to the "anthropometry" of the child will build his sense of independence because he can surmount challenges without relying on a grown-up to boost him up to decks that are too high or to provide a steadying hand on ladders that are too steep.

The key design areas for young children are handrails, climbing and footing details: Handrails should be at hand height and easily graspable — a height of 23-5/8" to 27-7/8" (60 to 70cm) and diameter of 1-5/8" to 1-3/4" (40 to 50mm). The distance between parallel hand rails on two sides of steps, bridges, slide entries and the like should be between 15-3/4" and 19-3/4" apart (40 to 50cm) so that the child can securely grasp both rails.

Steps and gaps between platforms should be between 5-7/8" and 9-7/8" (15 and 25cm) with the space between steps or platforms enclosed or filled in to prevent the child slipping through. Ladders should be propped at a 75-degree angle.

Attention should be paid to making decks and all walking surfaces non-slip. Round logs create an uneven surface and cause many falls. Flat timbers with narrow gaps is best. Keep in mind average foot dimensions: 4-7/8" x 2" (12.5 x 5cm) for a 20-month-old toddler. And to prevent head entrapment, be sure there are no gaps between 4" and 10" in ladders, raised decks or railings.

Table 1
Average Dimensions of Preschool Children
(all measurements are in inches)

Age	Height	Vertical Reach	Chest Height	Hip Height	Hand Length	Knee Height
2 - 3	36-3/4	42-1/4	25-5/8	15-7/8	4-1/8	8-3/4
3 - 4	39-7/8	45-7/8	28-3/8	18-3/16	4-1/2	9-7/16
4 - 5	42-5/8	49-5/8	30-15/16	19-7/8	4-3/4	10-3/8

Table 2
Average Dimensions of Toddlers
(all measurements are in inches)

Age	Height	Hip Height	Knee Height	Hand Length	Foot Length	Foot Width
12-15 mo.	30-1/8	13-7/8	8-1/8	3-5/8	4-5/8	1-15/16
16-19 mo.	31-1/4	14-3/4	8-1/2	3-11/16	4-3/4	2
20-23 mo.	32-1/2	16	9-1/8	3-3/4	4-15/16	2-1/8

Reprinted with permission from The Playground Network, Vancouver, Canada

Bibliography

Alberta Recreation and Parks. *Play Space Safety*, Recreation Development Division (mailing address: 9th Floor, Standard Life Center, 10405 Jasper Ave., Edmonton, Alberta, Canada, T5J 3N4).

Allison, Linda. *The Reasons for Seasons*, Little, Brown and Company, Boston & Toronto, 1975.

Beckwith, Jay. *Make Your Backyard More Interesting Than TV*, McGraw-Hill Book Co. and The San Francisco Book Co.,1980.

Boeschen, John. *Successful Playhouses*, Structures Publishing Co., Farmington, Michigan, 1979. (Box 1002, Farmington, Mich. 48024).

Burton, Leon and Kathy Kuroda. *ArtsPlay*, Addison-Wesley Publishing Co., 1981.

Caney, Steven. *Steven Caney's Play Book*, Workman Publishing Co., New York, 1975. (231 East 51st St. New York, NY 10022)

Cherry, Clare. *Creative Play for the Developing Child*, Fearon Pitman Publishers, Belmont California, 1976.

Cooper, Elizabeth K. *Science In Your Own Back Yard*, Harcourt, Brace & World, Inc., 1958.

Ellis, Margaret and A. Brian Nielsen. *Improvised Play Things* , The University of Alberta Press, Canada, 1980. (Edmonton, Alta.)

Fisher, Timothy. *Huts, Hovels & Houses*, Addison-Wesley Publishing Co., 1977.

Fluegelman, Andrew (editor). *The New Games Book*, The Headlands Press, Tiburon, California, 1976.

Gallahue, David L. *Developmental Play Equipment for Home and School*, John Wiley & Sons, 1975.

Hendricks, Barbara (editor). *A Safe Place to Play: Guidelines for Safe Public Playgrounds*, The Playground Network, Vancouver, Canada, 1985. (Box 58343, Stn. L, Vancouver, B.C. V6P 6E4)

Hill, Polly. *Children and Space*, a series of four articles reprinted from Habitat, a bimonthly magazine of Canada Mortgage and Housing Corporation, 1971.

Hill, Polly (advisor). *Play Spaces for Preschoolers* and *Play Opportunities for School-Age Children*, Canada Mortgage and Housing Corporation, 1980.

Hogan, Paul. *The Nuts and Bolts of Playground Construction*, Vol. 3 of *A Trilogy of Play*, Leisure Press, West Point, New York, 1982.

Hurtwood, Lady Allen of. *Planning for Play*, Thames and Hudson, London, 1975.

Mason, John. *The Environment of Play*, Vol. 2 of *A Trilogy of Play*, Leisure Press, West Point, New York, 1982.

Opie, Iona and Peter. *Children's Games in Street and Playground*, Oxford at the Clarendon Press, 1969.

Orlick, Terry. *The Cooperative Sports & Games Book*, Pantheon Books, New York, 1978.

Root, Jill. *Play Without Pain: A Manual for Playground Safety*, Child Accident Prevention Foundation of Australia, Melbourne, 1983. (Order from College Of Surgeon's Gardens, Spring Street, Melbourne, Australia.)

Sunset Books. *Sunset Ideas for Children's Rooms & Play Yards*, Lane Publishing Co., Menlo Park, California, 1980. (94025)

Walker, Les. *Housebuilding for Children*, The Overlook Press, Woodstock, New York, 1977.